# The
# Georgia Colony

by Dennis Brindell Fradin

 CHILDRENS PRESS®
CHICAGO

**Library of Congress Cataloging-in-Publication Data**

Fradin, Dennis B.
    The Georgia colony / by Dennis B. Fradin.
      p.  cm.
    Includes index.
    Summary: A historical account of Georgia's early days, from its creation as
a colony for debtors in the 1700s until its admission as the fourth state in
1788.
    ISBN 0-516-00392-5
    1. Georgia—History—Colonial period, ca. 1600-1775—Juvenile literature.
[1. Georgia—History—Colonial period, ca. 1600-1775.] I. Title.
F289.F8   1989
975.8'02—dc20
                                                89-34954
                                                    CIP
                                                       AC

1 2 3 4 5 6 7 8 9 10 R 98 97 96 95 94 93 92 91 90

# Table of Contents

In Georgia, peaches are an important, money-making crop. Panoramic view of the mountains and valleys of Cloudland Canyon (below).

# Chapter I

## The Empire State of the South

*The Most Delightful Country of the Universe*

> *Sir Robert Montgomery, describing the land that became Georgia in a book published in England in 1717*

Georgia is a state in the southeastern United States. Among the fifty states, Georgia is about average size. Yet Georgia is the largest of the twenty-six states east of the Mississippi River.

Georgia is in the region of the United States that people call "the South." Five other Southern states are Georgia's neighbors. Florida, in the country's southeastern tip, is to Georgia's south and to a small portion of the west. Alabama is Georgia's main neighbor to the west. Tennessee and North Carolina are to the north. South Carolina and a hundred-mile stretch of the Atlantic Ocean are to Georgia's east.

Georgia was one of England's thirteen American colonies, all of which lay on or near the Atlantic Ocean. The other twelve colonies—

State Seal of Georgia

Virginia, Massachusetts, New Hampshire, New York, Connecticut, Maryland, Rhode Island, Delaware, Pennsylvania, North Carolina, New Jersey, and South Carolina—were all founded or taken over by England between 1607 and 1670. Georgia, the last of the Thirteen Colonies, was not settled until 1733.

The Georgia Colony was created upon a great idea. During the early 1700s, tens of thousands of people in England who could not pay their debts were thrown in jail. Many stayed there for years, and some died there. A great Englishman named James Oglethorpe thought that, instead of rotting in jail, debtors should be given another chance. One reason he and other English people founded Georgia was as a place where debtors could start life fresh.

At its birth, Georgia was run on several other good principles. The other twelve colonies allowed slavery. At first, James Oglethorpe and Georgia's other founders banned slavery in their colony. Oglethorpe also tried to be fair to the Indians, and for many years the Native Americans and the Georgians got along rather well.

There was tremendous excitement in England about Georgia during the early 1730s. Books were written and sermons preached about this new colony that admitted debtors, banned slavery, and befriended the Indians. But in time these principles were ignored or forgotten, and Georgia became like the other colonies. Few debtors went to Georgia. Slavery was soon allowed in the colony. And—as had occurred in the other colonies—Georgians pushed the Indians off their lands.

By the 1770s, Georgia was a successful colony where nearly everyone farmed. Some colonists had large farms called plantations where black slaves did the work. Other families had smaller farms where they grew enough food to support themselves. Except for the slaves, most Georgians were satisfied with their way of life. For the most part, Georgians were not angered by the taxes that England imposed on the American colonies during the 1760s and 1770s.

In other colonies, though, the majority of the colonists were very angry over these taxes. In 1775, the Revolutionary War broke out between the American colonists and their English rulers. Of all thirteen colonies, Georgia was thought to have had the highest percentage of people who were loyal to England during this war. However, many Georgians, especially among the younger generation, fought on the American side during the Revolution. They helped free the colonies,

COLONIAL AMERICA

which began calling themselves the United States, from England.

Soon after the Revolutionary War, cotton, grown largely by slave labor, became Georgia's biggest crop. By 1826, Georgia was the leading cotton producer in the world. But by the mid-1800s, most Southerners were disagreeing with Northerners over slavery and other issues. The Southerners saw that the federal government was taking steps to end slavery. Georgia and other Southern states broke away and formed their own country—the Confederate States of America.

Between 1861 and 1865, Georgia and the other Confederate States fought the Union forces in the Civil War. For a while it appeared that the South would win, but the Union had more soldiers and supplies, and ultimately came out victorious. Near the end of the war, Union forces burned the city of Atlanta and destroyed a great deal of property in Georgia. The state was left in such shambles that Georgians had to work many years to rebuild it.

Georgia was mainly a farming region for its first two centuries. Even Georgia's nickname reflected this. Georgia was called the Peach State because of all the peaches its farmers grew. It also was called the Goober State because of all the peanuts (nicknamed "goobers") grown there. However,

Peanuts are nicknamed "goobers."

Wood products and textiles are manufactured in Georgia factories.

during the 1900s, a big change took place in Georgia. The state was still a leader in growing peanuts, peaches, and other farm products. But more and more factories opened. Since the 1950s, more Georgians have earned their living in factories than on farms.

Today, Georgia is a major producer of textiles (cloth goods), chemicals, paper and other wood products, packaged foods, airplanes, and auto bodies. Many of the factories are in Atlanta (Georgia's capital and largest city) and the state's other major cities. Thanks to all its factories and businesses, Georgia's main nickname today is the Empire State of the South.

Dr. Martin Luther
King, Jr.

Margaret Mitchell

Ty Cobb

The Empire State of the South has been home to some remarkable people. One of the towering figures of colonial America, James Oglethorpe, was born in England but lived for over six years in Georgia. Nearly two hundred years after Oglethorpe founded the Georgia Colony, one of the greatest people of the twentieth century was born in the state. His name was Dr. Martin Luther King, Jr. (1929–1968), and he was born in Atlanta. Dr. King worked to gain civil rights for African-Americans. For doing so, he won the 1964 Nobel Peace Prize.

Georgia has produced an amazingly large number of great writers. Margaret Mitchell (1900–1949), author of the famous Civil War novel *Gone with the Wind*, was born in the city of Atlanta. The wonderful writer Carson McCullers (1917–1967), was born in Columbus, Georgia. She was the author of the great novels *The Member of the Wedding* and *The Heart Is a Lonely Hunter*. Among Georgia's other superb authors were the poets Sidney Lanier (1842–1881) and Conrad Aiken (1889–1973).

A number of famous athletes have also hailed from Georgia. Ty Cobb (1886–1961), was born in Banks County, Georgia. Nicknamed "the Georgia Peach," Cobb had the highest lifetime batting

10

average (.367) in big-league baseball history. Bobby Jones (1902–1971), one of the great names in golf, was born in Atlanta.

Other famous Georgians have included a president, a discoverer, and the founder of the Girl Scouts in America. The president was Jimmy Carter, who was born in the small town of Plains, Georgia, in 1924. As the thirty-ninth president, Carter became known as a man of peace and an advocate for human rights. The discoverer was a small-town doctor named Crawford Williamson Long (1815–1878), who was born in Danielsville, Georgia. During the 1840s, Dr. Long discovered the use of *anesthetics*—substances that help patients lose feeling during operations. This discovery revolutionized surgery, which until then had often been horribly painful. The founder of the Girl Scouts in America was Juliette Gordon Low (1860–1927), who was born in Savannah, Georgia.

Jimmy Carter

Crawford Long

Juliette Low visits a group of Girl Guides in England.

The Okefenokee Swamp (above) is a wildlife refuge for birds, mammals, reptiles, fish, and amphibians, such as the American alligator (left).

Georgia also has some remarkable scenery. Along its Atlantic coast it has lovely beaches and islands. Inland it has vast forests of pines and other trees (two-thirds of Georgia is wooded) where such animals as bears and deer still live. Rising up out of the northern part of Georgia are the beautiful Appalachian Mountains. In the southeast is the famed Okefenokee Swamp—

home to alligators, wildcats, bears, deer, and many unusual kinds of birds.

For those who like history, the Empire State of the South is one of the most interesting places in the United States to visit. Battlefields where Northern and Southern troops clashed during the Civil War can be seen. Savannah—the first town founded by James Oglethorpe and his fellow English colonists—has sites dating from colonial days. Georgia also has a number of relics left by Indians dating back much earlier than colonial times. Since they were the people who were there first, it is with the Indians that we begin our story of colonial Georgia.

At John's Mill, visitors may see how water power was used to grind corn, wheat, and rye in the late 1800s.

The Etowah Indian Mounds
exhibit Indian sculpture. The
Etowah Indians lived here between
1000 A.D. and 1500 A.D.

The Ocmulgee National Monument
is the largest example of ancient
Indian civilization in the East. Its
earth lodges and mounds show
visitors how Indians lived here for
thousands of years.

# Chapter II

# The Indians of Georgia

*The English live worse than the Indians who are a more innocent people.*

> *Comment by Tomochichi, a great Indian chief of Georgia, when he visited England*

## THE MOUND BUILDERS

About 3,000 years ago, Indians called Mound Builders lived in much of what is now the eastern United States, including Georgia. We call them Mound Builders because they left thousands of dirt mounds, some of them very large.

The mounds had various purposes. Some were used for burying the dead. Skeletons have been found inside them. Other mounds were built in the shape of giant animals such as birds and snakes. They probably had a religious meaning. Still other mounds had temples and other important buildings on them.

The Mound Builders were farmers and hunters. They grew corn, tobacco, and other crops. They hunted deer and other wild animals. They ate the meat, and made clothing out of the skins. The Mound Builders were also talented artists. Many fascinating pieces of their pottery, stone sculpture, and masks have been found inside the mounds.

Georgia has several fascinating mounds. Near Cartersville in northwestern Georgia are the famed Etowah Mounds. They consist of three large mounds and several smaller ones. Temples and buildings probably once stood on top of the large mounds at Etowah, and hundreds of skeletons have been found inside one of the large mounds. Some tools and other items found at the Etowah Mounds were made of materials that could only be obtained hundreds of miles from Georgia. This proves that the Etowah Mound Builders traveled long distances to other parts of America and possibly traded with other Indians.

Many other mounds can be seen at Ocmulgee National Monument, near Macon, and in other parts of Georgia. The Rock Eagle Mound, near Eatonton in central Georgia, is one of the most interesting Mound Builder relics in the country. This mound is made of piled-up rocks in the shape of an eagle. It is 120 feet wide from wingtip to wingtip and 102 feet long from head to tail. Why did the Mound Builders make this huge eagle?

The giant Rock Eagle is believed to be over 5,000 years old. The eagle measures 102 feet from head to tail, and 120 feet from wingtip to wingtip.

Perhaps they thought their gods would like to look down upon the Earth and see the giant Rock Eagle.

### THE CREEKS AND THE CHEROKEES

Several hundred years ago, the Mound Builders' civilization ended. These prehistoric Indians were followed by the modern Indian tribes. In many cases, these modern tribes were descendants of the Mound Builders. This may have been the case with Georgia's two main Indian groups—the

Indian tribes surrounded their villages with tall, wooden fences called palisades.

Creeks and the Cherokees. The Creeks may have been descended from the Mound Builders who had lived in what is now the southern United States. The Cherokees may have been related to Mound Builders who had lived in Ohio.

The Creeks were not a single tribe but a confederation of related tribes that lived in what are now Alabama and Georgia. In Georgia, they lived mainly in the south. The Creeks called themselves the Muskogee. The English people who arrived later called them Creeks because they built their villages along creeks and rivers.

Several hundred people lived in a typical Creek village, which had a public square surrounded by homes and public buildings. Most families had two houses—one for winter and another for summer. The buildings were made of sticks, mud, poles, and tree bark. Many Creek villages were protected by tall wooden fences called palisades.

Like many other Indian tribes, the Creeks were farmers. They differed in one way from most other farming tribes, though. In most other tribes, men avoided farming, which was considered women's work. With the Creeks, the whole family farmed together. Corn, beans, squash, sweet potatoes, and pumpkins were their main crops. Each family harvested a portion of the crops for themselves. Another portion was stored by the village for the hard times of winter.

Storehouses were built of stones and earth.

Other work was divided between men and women. Creek men killed deer, buffalo, bears, wild turkeys, and other animals with bows and arrows, blowguns, and traps. Using poles and nets, they caught many kinds of fish in creeks and rivers. It was the women's work to cook the food and make clothes out of the animal skins. The women also did most of the child rearing. As for the children, girls helped their mothers with their work and boys helped their fathers.

By European standards, the Creeks could be very generous and very cruel. Guests, even strangers, were treated like family. They were fed the best foods and given a good place to sleep. On the other hand, the Creeks thought that no torture was too cruel for their enemies. The English people who came to Georgia in the 1700s were puzzled by the Creeks' ways. The English tended to be distrustful of strangers, but less cruel to their enemies.

Each Creek town had a chief, called a *mico*. The *mico* lacked the power to order people to do things. He gave advice, which people could follow or ignore. A number of other people also helped decide many matters. Among them were old warriors called "beloved men" and old women called "beloved women."

Now and then Creeks from various towns gathered for a big meeting. This often happened when one of the Creek tribes was threatened by war. The representatives from the various Creek tribes would decide what to do.

Like other American Indians, the Creeks believed in many gods. They called their main god the "Master of Breath." According to Creek beliefs, at one time their people had lived within the Earth. They came up onto Earth's surface through a hole. But because the world was covered by fog, they could not see. While wandering in the fog, the Creek people were separated into smaller groups. These groups begged the Master of Breath to blow the fog away so they could see.

Feeling sorry for the people, the Master of Breath blew the fog away with mighty puffs. Happy that they could see one another, the various Creek groups swore that they would always be like one large family.

The Master of Breath was supreme, but the Creeks believed in many other gods and spirits. The sun, moon, and planets were among their other important gods. Lesser spirits were thought to live in trees, lakes, and rivers.

To honor their gods, the Creeks held several yearly festivals during which they prayed, danced,

Food was an important part of Indian celebrations.

and feasted. The biggest one was the Green Corn Dance, which was held in July or early August. At this festival, the Creeks thanked the gods for helping the corn grow. The Green Corn Dance also marked the end of one year and the start of another. The Creeks let their sacred fire go out on the last day of the Green Corn Dance. They started a new fire to bring in the new year. With the start of the new fire, people were supposed to forget old grudges and make a fresh start with their enemies.

The Creeks loved games and enjoyed sports. One popular game resembled lacrosse. Goalposts made from thin tree trunks were set up on both sides of a long field. The purpose of the game was to send a small deerskin ball between the goalposts. Using sticks with a leather web on the end, the players passed the ball. They were even allowed to carry the ball in their mouths. This game was called "Brother to War" because it was so rough. What made it brutal was that players were allowed to hit each other with the sticks and even punch each other. One town often played another in "Brother to War." There was a less violent form of the game that men and women played together.

Another Creek game was called "chunkey." A yard for playing chunkey was an important part of a Creek village. A disk-shaped stone was rolled across the chunkey-yard. The players tried to strike the moving stone with their spears.

Georgia's other main Indian group was the Cherokee tribe. The Cherokees lived in the mountainous regions of the Carolinas, Virginia, Tennessee, Alabama, and Georgia. In Georgia they lived mainly in the north. The Cherokees called themselves *Ani-yun-wiya*—"the Real People." The name Cherokee, by which they are known to history, was probably given to them by the Creek Indians. It is thought to mean "People of a Different Language."

Despite their different language, the Cherokees resembled the Creeks in many ways. Several hundred people lived in a Cherokee village, which contained houses made of poles covered by bark. The Cherokees obtained their food by farming, hunting, and fishing. They worshiped many gods, and even had a Green Corn Dance.

But the Cherokees differed from their Creek neighbors to the south in some ways. Although Cherokee men cleared the fields, the women did all the work involved in growing the corn, beans, and squash. Yet women had special importance to the Cherokees. Although men were the tribal chiefs, the mothers headed the Cherokee families. Cherokee children were taught to call all younger women "Mother" and all older women "Grandmother." Cherokee women were often the village doctors. And Cherokee women were famous for making baskets which they dyed with berry juice.

The Cherokees' Green Corn Dance did not mark their new year. The Cherokee new year came several months later in November. Like the Creeks, the Cherokees killed the sacred fire that had burned all year. As the new fire was lit, people

This engraving by John White, an early explorer in the Carolina region, pictures an Indian dance.

were supposed to put aside their hatreds and start fresh. Another Cherokee ceremony was called the Booger Dance, when adults put on masks and danced around the fire until the children guessed who they were.

The Cherokees also played a ball game that resembled lacrosse, and a hoop-and-pole game that was similar to chunkey. A hoop, made of woven grass, was rolled along the ground. As the hoop tumbled around, the players tried to hurl poles through it.

The Cherokees believed in many animal gods, some of whom figured in their creation story. Long ago our world was covered by water, the Cherokees believed. In those olden times the animal gods lived on a platform in the sky world. When it became too crowded there, the animals sent the Great Water Beetle down to make the world habitable.

Water Beetle swam down into the water world and brought up some mud that became the land. The Great Buzzard then flew over the muddy land on an exploring trip. In places he flew too low. His wings beat up ridges that became the mountains. When the Cherokee people appeared, they settled in the mountains that the Great Buzzard had created.

A great deal of important history regarding the Creeks and the Cherokees took place in the 1800s, after the colonial period. The Cherokees' and the Creeks' lands kept shrinking as the Americans took more and more of it. The Creeks fought back, but the more numerous and better-armed Americans beat them in the Creek War of 1813–14. The Americans even got the Cherokees to help them

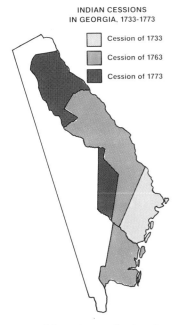

INDIAN CESSIONS
IN GEORGIA, 1733-1773

▫ Cession of 1733
▨ Cession of 1763
■ Cession of 1773

Map shows the lands that the Indians were forced to give up between 1733 and 1773.

26

Sequoya (left) invented the Cherokee alphabet (above).

win this war. In the 1830s, the surviving Creeks were forced to move out of Georgia into Oklahoma.

Meanwhile, the Cherokees had developed a civilization that resembled that of the Americans. In 1821, the Cherokee Indian Sequoya developed a writing system for his people. The Cherokees

27

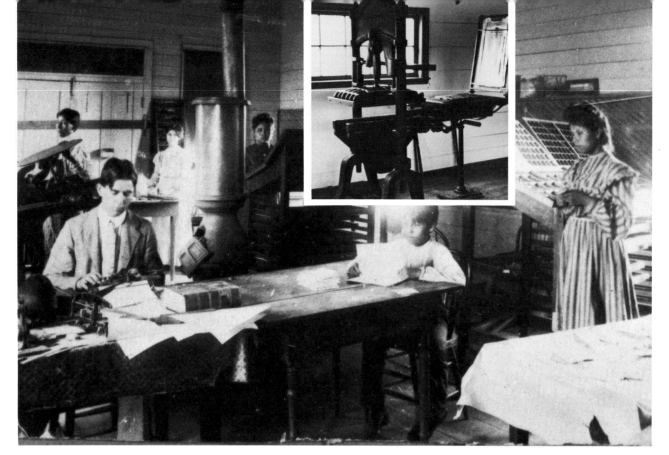

This photograph of the Cherokee print shop was taken in 1909. The press (inset), used to print the Cherokee newspaper, can be seen at New Echota, the capital of the Cherokee Indian Nation from 1825 to 1838.

then published books and newspapers in their own language, and opened schools where their children learned to read and write. The Cherokees thought that, because they lived much like the white people, they would be allowed to live side by side with them. But the Americans wanted the Cherokees' remaining lands.

About the time that the Creeks were driven out, the Cherokees also were forced to move from Georgia to Oklahoma. Since many Cherokees, Creeks, and other Indians who were kicked out of their homes at this time died on the journey to

Oklahoma, the trip became known as the "Trail of Tears."

One thing that made this mistreatment of Georgia's Indians in the 1800s especially sad was that Native Americans had helped the English found the Georgia Colony during the 1700s. Today, only about 10,000 Indians live in Georgia, most of them Creeks and Cherokees who have returned to the state.

Creek Indian

James Vann, an important Cherokee chief, built this house in 1804.

The voyages of Christopher Columbus (right) led to the colonization of land in the Americas by the Spanish, the French, and the English.

Christopher Columbus and his men sailed across the Atlantic Ocean in three ships—the *Niña*, the *Pinta*, and the *Santa Maria*.

# Chapter III

# The Spanish, the French, and the English

*Nature has not blessed the world with any tract which can be preferable to it [Georgia].*

*Sir Robert Montgomery (1717)*

## THE SPANISH AND THE FRENCH

In 1492, the queen and king of Spain sent Christopher Columbus on a voyage of exploration. Columbus was searching for a way to sail west to Asia. Columbus's path was blocked by land that he had not known was there—the Americas. It cannot be said that Columbus "discovered" the Americas, because Vikings (Norwegians and other Scandinavians) had reached the Americas about 1000 A.D. However, Columbus's famous voyage led to the first colonization of the Americas by the Spanish.

Spain was eager to colonize the New World for several reasons. The Spanish wanted to find gold and build towns and plantations in the Americas. In addition, they wanted to make the Indians

Preachers told the
Indians about
Christianity.

become Christians. In the process of taking over
new lands and bringing Christianity to the
natives, the Spanish made the Indians slaves.

The Spanish built the first European town in
the Americas just four years after Christopher
Columbus's famous voyage. This town was Santo
Domingo, on the island country of the Dominican
Republic. The oldest European-built city in the

Western Hemisphere, Santo Domingo was founded in 1496 by Christopher's brother, Bartholomew Columbus.

The Spanish soon built other settlements along the east coast of the Americas. They began to colonize Cuba in 1511, Mexico in 1519, and Colombia in 1525. The Spanish grew rich from the gold and other treasures they found in the Americas. But the Spanish conquest was purely evil as far as the American Indian people were concerned. Hundreds of thousands of them were enslaved or killed by the Spanish conquerors.

In the early 1500s, Spain became interested in Florida, just south of Georgia. In 1513, the Spanish explorer Juan Ponce de León came to Florida searching for the Fountain of Youth. The fountain's waters supposedly could make old people young. Ponce de León did not find the Fountain of Youth (because it never existed), but he did begin the exploration of the present-day southeastern United States.

Most other Spanish explorers had more interest in the gleaming yellow metal—gold—than in magic waters. In 1528, the Spaniard Pánfilo de Narváez led a large expedition into Florida in search of gold. The men were shipwrecked and many of them died. A few years later, the Spaniard

Hernando de Soto made a long exploration of the southeastern United States in quest of gold. During this trip, he became the first known non-Indian to set foot in Georgia.

It was spring of 1539 when Hernando de Soto sailed from Cuba to the mainland of what is now the United States. De Soto and his six hundred men landed at Tampa Bay and marched northward. As they did so, they kidnapped Indians and made them work for them. Chained together and poorly fed, many of these Indians died.

The DeSoto expedition explored the southeastern part of what is now the United States of America.

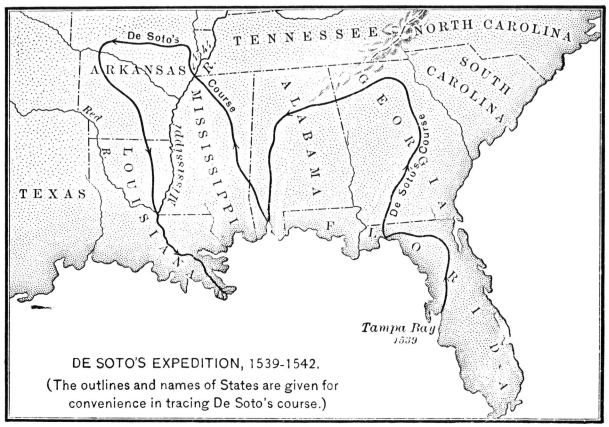

DE SOTO'S EXPEDITION, 1539-1542.

(The outlines and names of States are given for convenience in tracing De Soto's course.)

Map shows the route taken by the DeSoto expedition from 1539 to 1542.

De Soto and his men entered present-day Georgia perhaps near what is now the city of Valdosta in the far southern part of the state. They spent four months marching northeast across Georgia. De Soto found no gold in Georgia, nor did he find it elsewhere on this trip. The Creek Indians, well known for their hospitality, brought food to de Soto and his men when they were in Georgia. In return, de Soto captured some Creeks and added them to his slave crew.

Darley.

DeSoto and his men made slaves of the Indians.

The march across Georgia brought de Soto and his men to about where the city of Augusta now stands. Then they crossed the Savannah River into present-day South Carolina. This long expedition ended for Hernando de Soto in the spring of 1542 when he died on the Mississippi River at the boundary of what are now the states of Louisiana and Mississippi. De Soto's body was buried in the river.

Even though they had found no gold there, the Spanish wanted to add what is now the southeastern United States to their list of American possessions. At this time, France was also interested in the region of Florida, Georgia, and the Carolinas. In 1564, the French had tried to settle Florida, but the Spanish drove them out. In 1565, the Spanish built St. Augustine, Florida— the first permanent European town in what is now the United States. In order to get a stronger hold on the region, Spain built forts along the coast of what is now the southeastern United States. In 1566, the Spanish built a fort on St. Catherines Island in what is now Georgia. A few years later, Spanish priests built missions in Georgia where they taught the Indians about Christianity.

We are using the name Georgia because that is the name by which the colony and then the state were later known. But back when the Spanish were building missions and other outposts in Georgia, they called the region *Guale*. That was the name of a local Indian chief.

Although Spain and France would have liked to gain control over the east coast of what is now the United States, neither country did much about settling the region. The French preferred trading for furs to building farms and towns. Except for Florida, the Spanish showed little interest in building settlements along the east coast. Although Spain claimed the Georgia region, only a few Spanish people lived in what is now Georgia during the late 1500s and early 1600s.

## THE ENGLISH START BUILDING THE THIRTEEN COLONIES

In the early 1600s, a people who were eager to build farms and towns began coming to America. These were the English. In 1607, the English built their first permanent town in their first permanent colony in America. It was Jamestown in the Virginia Colony.

English people had several reasons for moving to America. During the 1600s, England did not offer freedom of religion. Some English families came to America so they could worship as they pleased. The Pilgrims who settled Massachusetts in 1620 came in search of religious liberty. Other English people came to America because they could have more land here than they could in the "mother country." Still others had experienced problems in England and were searching for a place to make a fresh start.

England ruled the American Colonies and provided most of the population. But people from Germany, Scotland, Ireland, and other European countries also settled in the colonies. By 1670, England ruled twelve American Colonies, which were home to about 110,000 settlers. By then the Florida-Georgia region was the only part of what is now the United States east coast not under English control.

Spain had control of Florida, but only a weak hold on Georgia. England had claimed the Georgia region for itself as early as 1629, but a century passed before the English tried to back up their claim. In fact, not until the Englishman James Oglethorpe had a grand idea in the early 1700s did Georgia come under English rule.

*To all to whom these Presents shall come.*

Whereas his Majesty hath been graciously pleas'd to take into consideration that many of his poor Subjects, & many Forreigners, who are willing to become his Subjects, are reduced to great Necessities, & would gladly be settled in the British Provinces in America, where by Cultivating the Lands at present vast & desolate, they might not only gain a comfortable Subsistence for themselves & families, but also strengthen his Majesty's Colonies & encrease the Trade, Navigation & Wealth of these Realms.

And Whereas his Majesty hath declared it highly becoming his Crown & Royal Dignity to extend his Fatherly Compassion even to the meanest & most unfortunate of his People, & to releive the Wants of his abovementioned poor Subjects, & that it will be highly conducive for the Accomplishing these Ends, that a regular Colony of the said poor People be settled & established in the Southern Frontiers of South Carolina, And Whereas his Majesty for the more orderly Carrying on the said good Purposes Hath by his Royal Charter bearing Date the Ninth Day of June A.D. 1732 constituted a Body Politick & Corporate by the Name of The Trustees for Establishing the Colony of GEORGIA in AMERICA & hath granted unto the said Trustees, & their Successors for ever certain Lands & Territories in South Carolina, In trust for Establishing the said Colony, & hath erected the same into an independent Province by the Name of GEORGIA: Now know Ye that we the said Trustees being well assured of the Integrity & Humanity of Charles Dubois Esquire & that he greatly desireth the Success and Accomplishment of so excellent a Work, Have by Vertue of the Powers granted to us by the said Charter, at a Meeting of the said Corporation convened & assembled for that Purpose, authorized & appointed, and by these presents Do for the Considerations aforesaid, authorize & appoint the said Charles Dubois Esquire to take Subscriptions & to gather & collect such Moneys, as shall be by any Person or Persons contributed for the Purposes aforesaid, & to transmit with all convenient Speed, to us the said Trustees, at our Office in old Palace Yard Westminster, the Moneys so collected, together with the Names of the Persons & Sums wch. each one shall contribute or subscribe, & in case any of ye Contributors shall desire their Names to be conceal'd, then the Sums by them given respectively, in order that we the said Trustees may be enabled from time to time to publish perfect Accounts of such Benefactions. —— Given under our common Seal this Tenth Day of August 1732.

This document asked for funds to support the Georgia Colony.

# Chapter IV

# The Founding of the Georgia Colony

*The river here forms a half-moon, around the south side of which the banks are about forty feet high, and on the top a flat, which they call a bluff. The plain, high ground extends into the country about five or six miles, and along the river for about a mile. . . . Upon the riverside, in the center of the plain, I have laid out the town. . . . The river is pretty wide, the water fresh. . . . For about six miles up into the country the landscape is very agreeable, the stream being wide and bordered with high woods on both sides.*

*From a letter written in February of 1733 by James Oglethorpe, who had just founded Savannah, the first town in the Georgia Colony*

### THE GREAT IDEA

According to English laws of the early 1700s, people who owed large sums of money could be jailed. The debtors' prisons were filthy places where many people died of disease. Those who tried to escape were tortured or chained to dead bodies. The hopeless part was that, once inside, people could not earn the money they needed to pay their debts.

The Reading Poor House was a debtors' prison in England.

James Edward
Oglethorpe

In the 1720s, a young man named James Edward Oglethorpe lived in England. A member of the British lawmaking body called the Parliament, Oglethorpe was a fighter for human rights. In 1728, he wrote a pamphlet protesting the practice of impressing sailors—kidnapping them and making them work on ships.

Also in 1728, a friend of Oglethorpe's named Robert Castell was jailed for not paying his debts. An architect and author, Castell was mistreated in debtors' prison, where he died.

James Oglethorpe was upset and angry about his friend's death. He demanded that Parliament do something about the debtors' prisons. Oglethorpe himself was appointed chairman of a committee to investigate. He helped make changes in the laws that resulted in the freeing of hundreds or perhaps thousands of debtors and the improvement of conditions in the debtors' prisons.

Freeing some debtors reduced, but did not solve, the problem. Many thousands of debtors were still in jail. And the freed debtors had trouble getting jobs in England, because they still owed money there.

In about 1729, Oglethorpe became friends with Dr. Thomas Bray, an Englishman who also was

During the reign of George II of England, debtors were kept in filthy rooms in Fleet Prison.

concerned about the country's poor. Dr. Bray may have helped plant a brilliant idea in Oglethorpe's mind, or perhaps Oglethorpe thought of it himself. In any event, James Oglethorpe began promoting a plan to ship debtors to America, where they could make a fresh start.

Dr. Bray died in early 1730, leaving a large sum of money to be used for charitable purposes. Oglethorpe spoke to other wealthy people and raised more money. He and his friends asked England's King George II to grant them land in America between the English Carolinas and the Spanish Florida. To flatter the king, they decided to name their colony Georgia, after him.

George II ruled from
1727 to 1760.

King George II and his aides saw that they could "kill three birds with one stone" by sending English debtors to Georgia. They could rid their country of debtors. They could make sure that the land between Florida and the Carolinas was settled by English people. And from Georgia they could watch the activities of the Spanish in Florida and the French in the huge territory of French Louisiana to the west. In spring of 1732, the king signed a charter creating a new colony called Georgia. Its government was to be in the hands of twenty-one men called Trustees.

In the early 1730s, a tremendous wave of excitement about Georgia swept England. All over the country people donated money to help found the Georgia Colony. Poets and preachers predicted that the new colony would be a "Garden of Eden" where people would live in harmony and prosper from farming.

Very soon, though, there was a change of plan. The original idea of providing a home for debtors was put aside, and in fact few debtors ever reached colonial Georgia. Instead, Georgia was to be settled mainly by people who were out of work and by foreigners who were persecuted due to their religion. Those people who were accepted as "charity" colonists would have their way paid by the Trustees. They would also receive fifty acres of land in Georgia and enough food and supplies to keep them going for a year. Although the Trustees wanted Georgia to be mainly a home for poorer small farmers, some people who could pay their own way—called "adventurers"—would also be admitted to the colony. They would be allowed five hundred acres of land—ten times as much as the "charity" colonists.

The Trustees placed notices in English newspapers saying that people who wished to live in Georgia should contact them. Of the hundreds who applied, about thirty-five families consisting of about 120 people were chosen for the first settlement of Georgia.

Seal of the Georgia Trustees

### THE TRIP TO AMERICA

On a fall day in 1732, the Georgia colonists boarded a ship called the *Anne* in Gravesend, England, near London. Of the twenty-one men who were Trustees, James Oglethorpe was the only one who was going to Georgia, and in fact he was the only Trustee who ever went there. On November 17, 1732, the *Anne* sailed down England's Thames River. Several days later, the ship reached the Atlantic Ocean. The *Anne* sailed down around England and then headed west—toward America.

It was very crowded aboard the ship. Besides the approximately 120 people, a large number of hogs, geese, ducks, and sheep were being brought to stock the farms. The people had to sleep in cradles that were just a bit over five and one-half feet long. The approximately twenty children on board may have slept comfortably, but the teen-agers and adults must have felt cramped.

Although Georgia had no official governor, the colonists considered Oglethorpe their leader. Just as young Cherokee Indians called all women "Mother," the colonists aboard the *Anne* all began to call Oglethorpe "Father." When there were arguments on the crowded ship, Oglethorpe settled them. On days when the weather allowed, Oglethorpe took all the men on deck and gave them military drills. Every man in the colony had to be ready to serve as a soldier in case of a clash with Spain or another foreign power. When a baby was born on board, Oglethorpe was named the godfather. The baby was named Georgius Marinus Warren after the new colony. Had it been a girl, the baby probably would have been named Georgia Marina Warren.

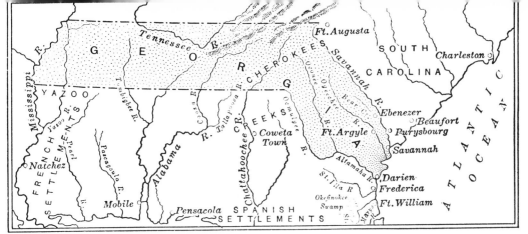

Map shows the land granted to the Georgia Trustees in 1732.

Dr. William Cox had agreed to serve as physician to the Georgia colonists for a year free of charge. Dr. Cox treated the colonists who became ill aboard the *Anne*. He must have done a good job, for the only deaths were two babies who had been sick upon the departure from England.

## FOUNDING SAVANNAH

On the morning of January 13, 1733, the people aboard the *Anne* spotted land. They had not sailed directly to Georgia, but had instead stopped at Charleston, South Carolina. The colonists were not allowed to leave the *Anne* and enter the town of Charleston. It was feared that they would like the town so much they would never want to leave! However, James Oglethorpe went ashore and met with South Carolina Governor Robert Johnson.

Oglethorpe showed Governor Johnson the Georgia charter and asked for his help. South Carolinians were thrilled about the settlement of Georgia, for it meant they would have a colony between themselves and the Spanish to the south. South Carolina lawmakers provided the new colony with cattle, pigs, a large amount of rice, and also boats for transportation.

The *Anne* continued southwest down South Carolina's Atlantic coast. The ship stopped off South Carolina's southern tip. For a few days the colonists visited with people in and around Beaufort, South Carolina. Meanwhile, James Oglethorpe went out looking for a site for Georgia's first town.

Because travel in the 1700s was mainly by water, nearly all major colonial towns were built near the ocean or along rivers. Oglethorpe explored along a river that South Carolina's Westo Indians had called *Westobou*, or "River of the Westos," and the Spaniards called *Rio Dulce*, or "Sweet River." The English called it the Savannah, after a small Indian tribe. Oglethorpe chose a place about eighteen miles up the Savannah River just over the border from South Carolina. The spot he picked was Yamacraw Bluff, which overlooked the river.

Oglethorpe liked Yamacraw Bluff for several reasons. He wanted Georgia's first town to be close to South Carolina for mutual protection. The nearby river could provide drinking water, and it was deep enough for large ships to come within thirty feet of the riverbank. There were plenty of tall trees nearby that could be cut down and used for building houses. High ground had fewer insects and was generally healthier than low ground. One other thing cinched it. An Indian village stood on the bluff. Oglethorpe knew that the Indians chose the best places for their villages.

Before the colonists could settle on this bluff, Oglethorpe had to get permission from the Indians who already lived there. These Indians had an interesting history. Under their Chief Tomochichi, they had for some unknown reason broken away from the Creek Confederacy and had moved from the Creek village of Coweta which stood several hundred miles to the west. Consisting of only about one hundred people, Tomochichi's band called themselves Yamacraws. They had been living at Yamacraw Bluff, which was named after them, for only several years when James Oglethorpe first visited them.

Near Tomochichi's village stood a trading post run by John and Mary Musgrove. John had come from South Carolina. His wife Mary was half Creek and half English and could speak both languages. With Mary translating, James

The first colonists land in Georgia.

Oglethorpe spoke to Tomochichi. Oglethorpe explained to the elderly chief that the colonists wanted to be friendly. Tomochichi generously said that the region had room for both Indians and settlers. He also said that his people would welcome the Georgia colonists. From that first meeting until his dying day, Tomochichi was a great friend of the Georgia Colony.

Oglethorpe went to South Carolina and returned with the rest of the colonists. They landed on February 12, 1733. People in the Savannah area still celebrate February 12 as the birthday of Georgia.

The settlers at first lived in tents while they built their town, which they named Savannah after the river and the Indian tribe. Savannah was one of the most carefully laid out United States cities. James Oglethorpe did the job with the help of Colonel William Bull, a South Carolina engineer.

Savannah was built with streets as straight as the lines on a football field. The main street was named Bull Street for William Bull. The straight

The plan of the city of Savannah, Georgia

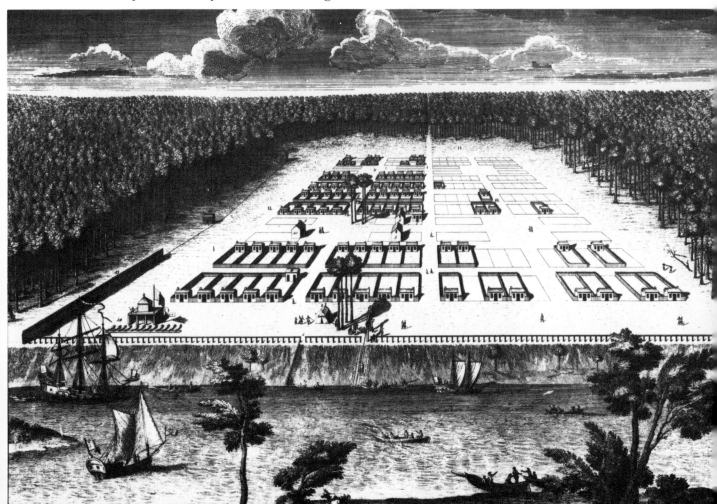

Early map of the county of Savannah

streets were interrupted here and there parks. Savannah's first square was Johnson Square, named for South Carolina's Governor Robert Johnson.

Each family was to have a home and a garden plot inside Savannah totaling five acres. They were to have another forty-five acres (the "adventurers" could have more) outside Savannah for their main farming grounds.

Pine trees were chopped down and the wood used to construct houses and military buildings. Room was also set aside for a Trustees' Garden. This was an experimental garden where experts would see which kinds of plants would grow well in Georgia.

Although Tomochichi and his Yamacraws had welcomed the Georgia colonists, it was crucial that the region's other Indians also accept them. An important meeting was organized in Savannah in May of 1733. At this meeting about fifty Creek *micos* and warriors gave the Georgia colonists permission to settle a large area between the Savannah and Altamaha rivers.

The colonists had expected life to be easy in Georgia. The talk about what a "Garden of Eden" Georgia would be had given many of them wrong ideas. They thought the land was so fertile that plenty of food could be grown without any trouble. They expected that two kinds of plants—grapes and mulberry trees—would bring them great wealth. The grapes would be made into wine and the mulberry trees would yield food for silkworms, which would then produce silk. The Georgians hoped to sell their wine and silk to Europe.

Georgia was not the land of plenty that the colonists had expected. The land around Savannah was not as fertile as they thought. Not only that, but the people were used to the mild climate of England, where summer temperatures were usually in the sixties and seventies. Savannah's summer temperatures often reached the nineties.

Their first summer in Savannah, many settlers came down with fever and other illnesses. William Cox, the doctor who had volunteered to serve the colony, was one of the first to die. That first summer alone, about forty of the Georgia colonists died. (This included some people who had come to Georgia after the arrival of the *Anne.*) The colony's first baby, Georgia Close, had been born in March of 1733. Before the end of the year, Georgia Close had died, too.

Fortunately, food was no problem that first year, or the death toll would have been even higher.

Food had been brought from England, and also supplied by the South Carolinians and the Indians. The colonists' gardens began producing some vegetables in that first year, too.

## OTHER NEWCOMERS

Soon after the founding of Savannah, more people moved to the new colony. Some moved down from the Carolinas. Others came by ship from England and other European countries. In July of 1733, a ship carrying Jewish people arrived in Savannah. Oglethorpe welcomed these Jewish colonists. Among them was a doctor named Samuel Nunes who cured many of the sick Georgians of their fevers.

There was strong prejudice in Europe against Jewish people at that time. When officials in London learned that Oglethorpe had welcomed Jewish people, they ordered him to evict them. Oglethorpe refused. Ever since that summer day in 1733 when the first families arrived, Savannah has had a relatively large Jewish population.

In early 1734, a group of German-speaking people called Salzburgers arrived in Georgia. These people were Protestants who had come from a region near what is now the German-Austrian border. Like the Jews, they had been persecuted in their homelands due to their religion. Even before the Salzburgers left their ship, James Oglethorpe brought them gifts of meat and vegetables. The Jewish people also helped the Salzburgers get started in Georgia. At first the Salzburgers settled at a town they called Ebenezer about twenty-five miles northwest of Savannah.

People from Scotland also came to Georgia in 1734. Scottish people built a town called Darien at the mouth of the Altamaha River, about sixty miles south of Savannah. Georgia was being settled, but in small numbers. By 1735, only several hundred colonists lived in Georgia, nearly all of them in or close to Savannah.

The Salzburgers left their homes and immigrated to the Georgia Colony.

# TOMOCHICHI (1650?–1739)

Little is known about Tomochichi's life until 1733, when he met and began helping James Oglethorpe and the first Georgia colonists. Even the place and year of Tomochichi's birth are not known for sure. Some say he was born around 1650 in the Indian village of Coweta, near present-day Columbus in far western Georgia. If that was the case, he was already about eighty years old when he befriended the colonists.

Only a few basic facts are known about Tomochichi's earlier life. We know that he married a woman named Senawki and that the two of them raised their nephew Tooanahowi as their son. We know that Tomochichi fought bravely in at least one war against another tribe. And although the reason is a mystery, we know that in the 1720s Tomochichi led about one hundred people away from Coweta to the spot where Savannah was later built. Tomochichi was the *mico* (chief) of this splinter group, which called itself the Yamacraw tribe.

Because the colonists left written records, we know more about the last six years of Tomochichi's life than we do about all his earlier years. By the time James Oglethorpe appeared on that February day in 1733, Tomochichi had become a man who would go to great lengths to keep the peace. He was also a friendly person, who saw no harm in offering the colonists a piece of land and his hospitality.

One of Tomochichi's finest traits was his willingness to adopt some of the colonists' ways while keeping his Indian identity. This trait came out in his views toward education and religion. Tomochichi soon concluded that formal schools like those of the Europeans would help his people. In 1735, he and some Georgians belonging to the Moravian religion founded an Indian school called Irene near Savannah. Mainly for Tomochichi's Yamacraws, Irene was one of the first schools in colonial Georgia. Children, as well as some adult Indians, learned to read and write in this three-room schoolhouse.

The missionaries who ran Irene and other colonists wanted Tomochichi and his people to become Christians. Tomochichi was curious about Christianity, but after learning about it he decided that his religion was better. He once remarked that he objected to the way Christians prayed to God for favors. "We do not pray to God in that way," Tomochichi said. "We leave it up to Him to do what He thinks best. The asking of any special blessing looks as if we were telling God what to do."

In 1734, Tomochichi, Senawki, their adopted son Tooanahowi, and several other Indians accompanied James Oglethorpe to England. People in England were impressed by Tomochichi's dignified, kindly, friendly, and generous manner. While in London, Tomochichi met the Georgia

Trustees. The old *mico* expressed his hope that his people would live in peace with the English. "Now that I am old, I wish to see my nation settled and prosperous before I die," he said in his own language. "I feel in my heart that the English are good people and we wish to live near them as good neighbors."

Tomochichi also met England's King George II and Queen Caroline on this visit. Giving the king a present of eagle feathers, Tomochichi said: "These are the feathers of the eagle which is the swiftest of birds. These feathers are a sign of peace in our land . . . and we have brought them over to leave with you, O Great King, as a sign of everlasting peace."

The English had wanted to impress Tomochichi with the glory of their civilization, so that the Indians would know that Georgia was backed by a mighty nation. Tomochichi was not as awed as the English had hoped. He saw that London was crowded and filthy and had many poor people. "The English live worse than the Indians who are a more innocent people," he commented.

Tomochichi and his friends and relatives returned to Georgia in late 1734. The great *mico* spent his last years settling disputes between Indians and colonists, helping James Oglethorpe in many ways, and ruling his people. He died in October of 1739, at what many people thought was about the age of ninety. As Tomochichi had requested, he was buried in Savannah, the town he had helped James Oglethorpe found.

---

## JAMES OGLETHORPE (1696–1785)

James Edward Oglethorpe was born in London into a prominent family. He was educated at Eton College and then at Oxford University. At the age of fourteen, he joined the English army and rose quickly to captain of the Queen's Guard.

In those days, many European regions that are now parts of countries were ruled by princes who kept private armies. Oglethorpe wanted to experience combat and visit foreign lands. He resigned from the English army at the age of nineteen and joined the Austrian army of Prince Eugene. Oglethorpe earned a reputation on the battlefield as a fine soldier.

A famous incident in the life of James Oglethorpe took place while he was serving Prince Eugene. One day Oglethorpe was dining with some important people. Suddenly a German prince splashed wine onto

Oglethorpe's face and pretended it was a joke. Oglethorpe couldn't yell at such an important man, but he was too proud to let the insult pass. "That's a good joke, but we do it much better in England," he said, throwing a whole glassful of wine at the prince's face. Fortunately the prince laughed, or Oglethorpe might have had to fight a duel.

James Oglethorpe made drastic changes in his life several times. Temporarily leaving the military life, at age twenty-six he won a seat in Parliament. There, this man who had a reputation as a fine soldier earned respect as a great humanitarian. He fought for the rights of sailors and prisoners, and also opposed slavery. He didn't just talk about his beliefs. He put them into action by founding Georgia as a refuge for the poor, and he was the only Trustee to ever set foot in the colony.

Nearly everyone who knew Oglethorpe respected him. Most of the colonists loved him and called him "Father." Not only did he spend a great deal of his own money on Georgia, he shared the hardships with the people. For example, in other colonies many of the leaders built houses for themselves before anyone else had a home. While Savannah was being built, Oglethorpe lived in a tent for almost a year to show that he wanted no special treatment.

Oglethorpe was also one of the few colonists who was liked and respected by the Indians. Tomochichi called Oglethorpe "the Great Man," and other Indians felt the same way about him. One time the Spanish were trying to convince a Creek chief to side with them against Oglethorpe and the colonists. "Oglethorpe is poor, he can give you nothing," said the Spanish. "It is foolish for you to go back to him."

"We love him," the Creek chief answered. "It is true he does not give us silver, but he gives us everything we want that he has. He has given me the coat off his back and the blanket from under him."

Sandwiched around two trips to England, Oglethorpe spent a total of over six years in the colony he had founded. During those years he brought more colonists to Georgia, kept the peace with the Indians, and defended the colony against the Spanish. In summer of 1743, he left Georgia for the last time. He returned to England to answer charges about how he had run the army in Georgia and to be repaid the money he had spent on the colony. The charges were dismissed and Oglethorpe was paid the money he was owed. Like Tomochichi, James Oglethorpe lived to be very old. When he died at his home in England at the age of eighty-eight, Oglethorpe was one of England's most famous people.

Portrait of Tomochichi and his adopted son, Tooanahowi (right). In 1743, Tomochichi, accompanied by his son and wife and several other Indians went to England.

# Chapter V

# The Young, Growing Colony

*Slavery is against the Gospel, as well as the fundamental law of England. We refused as trustees to make a law permitting such a horrid crime.*

*James Oglethorpe, founder of the Georgia Colony*

### A TRIP TO ENGLAND

In spring of 1734, James Oglethorpe returned to England to report to the Trustees and raise money for his Georgia colony. With him he took Tomochichi, Tomochichi's wife Senawki, their adopted son Tooanahowi, and several other Indians. John Musgrove acted as interpreter. They reached England after a two-month voyage.

In London, Tomochichi approved the treaty that the Creeks had made with the Georgia colonists. He also took steps to protect his people from being cheated by dishonest traders in Georgia, as was already happening.

James Oglethorpe also accomplished a great deal during his stay in the mother country.

Georgia was dependent on the approval of the Trustees and on money raised in England. Oglethorpe told the Trustees and the Parliament about the progress Georgia was making. He raised money for the colony, and lined up more colonists to go there, including ministers. He also worked out details for building a town on St. Simons Island along Georgia's southeastern coast.

In January of 1735, while Oglethorpe was still in England, the Trustees officially passed three rules for Georgia that had been in effect unofficially. There were to be no slaves in the colony. Rum was banned. And no colonist could trade with the Indians unless given special permission by the Trustees.

Oglethorpe disliked slavery, and had been the first to suggest that it be outlawed in Georgia. But the Trustees did not ban slavery just because it was evil. Some thought that the "adventurers" would be able to afford slaves while the poorer people couldn't, causing resentments. The ban on rum was Oglethorpe's idea, too. He wanted to avoid drunkenness among the colonists. He also was afraid that Georgians would get the Indians drunk and then cheat them in deals, as happened regularly in other colonies.

## ARGUMENTS, WAR, AND SLAVES

Oglethorpe sailed back to Georgia in late 1735 (the Indians having returned earlier). Coming to Georgia with Oglethorpe were a group of German-speaking people called Moravians, more Salzburgers, and the English ministers John and Charles Wesley.

John Wesley

A few years later, John Wesley would become a major figure in the history of religion by founding the Methodist Church. His brother Charles would become famous as a writer of Methodist hymns. But in 1735, the Wesley brothers were not yet famous. They came to Georgia for idealistic reasons. John Wesley wanted to serve as a missionary to the Indians. Charles was to preach and serve as James Oglethorpe's secretary of Indian affairs.

Oglethorpe had orders from England to build the town of Frederica on St. Simons Island. Located near present-day Georgia's southeastern border, Frederica was to be a military town from which Georgians could monitor the movements of the Spaniards to the south. In early 1736, Oglethorpe took some workmen to St. Simons Island and laid out Frederica. The colonists who went to live at Frederica were rowed there from

Charles Wesley

the mainland on boats. Finding the place beautiful and also because he wanted to be on hand in case of trouble with the Spanish, Oglethorpe built himself a cottage on St. Simons Island. Also under construction by 1736 was the town of Augusta, about one hundred miles northwest of Savannah.

Meanwhile, the Salzburgers at Ebenezer were enduring hard times. Their crops were doing poorly, heavy rains flooded the ground, and there was a great deal of illness in the town. The Salzburgers felt that they were too far from Savannah. In 1736, they asked Oglethorpe if they could move closer. Oglethorpe agreed, and the Salzburgers built a town called New Ebenezer just fifteen miles north of Savannah.

By the end of 1736, Georgia had five main towns—Savannah, New Ebenezer, Darien, Frederica, and Augusta. As the newest of the American colonies, Georgia naturally had the smallest population of the thirteen. But Georgia's population growth was much smaller than people had expected. By 1740, only about 2,000 colonists lived in Georgia. In contrast, Virginia, the most populous colony, had about 180,000 people (including slaves) by then. Even tiny Delaware, which had the lowest population except for Georgia, was home to about 20,000 people.

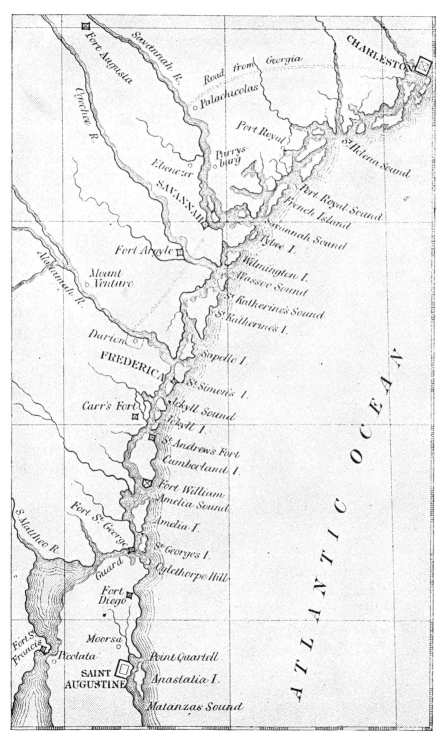

Map of the Georgia coastal settlements before 1743

Throughout history, people have planned "perfect" communities, only to see them turn out far from perfect due to human nature. Despite the lofty ideas behind its founding, Georgia had its share of the greed, jealousy, and fighting that often occurs among groups of people.

The experts who ran the Trustees' Garden argued bitterly with one another. One man even threatened another with a gun. After a few years, the experimental crop garden was abandoned, partly due to this bickering.

The Wesley brothers also became involved in bitter disputes. Within a short time, Charles, who was preaching at Frederica, was arguing with a number of the colonists. Charles thought that Georgians did not take religion seriously enough, and he quarreled with a man who fired a gun during a sermon. Charles returned to England after just a few months in Georgia.

Instead of working as a missionary among the Indians, John Wesley replaced a Savannah minister who had been fired after the colonists complained about him to the Trustees. John, too, had trouble with the Savannahians (as the people of Savannah are called). John fell in love with a young woman who married someone else. He then prevented the woman from taking part in religious activities. Although he claimed it was for religious reasons, many people felt he was doing it out of spite. A lawsuit was filed against John Wesley. The man who later founded the Methodist Church had all kinds of trouble until he finally left Georgia in late 1737.

The colonists never made the fortune from producing wine and silk that they had expected. Because of the difficulty of working in the heat and the expense of paying farm workers, it looked as if farming might never pay off for Georgians. Then some Georgians had an idea about how to make farming more profitable. They would have black slaves do the work, just as was done in other colonies.

A few Georgians, especially around Augusta, found ways around the colony's ban on owning slaves. Some pretended to "rent" slaves from South Carolina, which allowed slavery. Actually, these "rental" deals were made for such periods of time as one hundred years, meaning that in effect they had bought the slaves. Also, a few Georgians who owned second homes in South Carolina sneaked their slaves into Georgia.

As Georgians ripped down their colony's foundations from within, they were also threatened from the outside. During the 1700s, England had two main enemies—France and Spain. Between 1689 and 1763, England and France fought four wars over control of much of North America. These French and Indian Wars, which England finally won in 1763, involved mainly the Northern colonies.

In 1739, England began a war with its other main enemy, Spain, that involved Georgia. It was called the "War of Jenkins' Ear" (1739–1744), and it was sparked by a strange incident.

At the time, Spain controlled not only Florida but also other lands in present-day Central and South America including Mexico, Cuba, Colombia, and Panama. Spain wanted to keep other countries from trading with its colonies in the Americas. Without competition, Spain could take advantage of its colonies. Likewise, England wanted to be the only nation to trade with its Thirteen Colonies.

Both England and Spain had laws preventing their colonies from trading with other nations. These laws were hard to enforce. Ship captains from non-English countries smuggled goods into the Thirteen Colonies. Ship captains from non-Spanish nations smuggled goods into Spain's colonies to the south.

In 1731, an English ship captain called Robert Jenkins was smuggling goods to Spanish possessions on the islands off Florida. Spanish coast guards caught him and took goods from his ship. To punish Jenkins, they reportedly cut off one of his ears.

Jenkins claimed to have saved his ear for seven years. During that time, Spanish coast guards continued to seize British ships that came to trade with Spain's possessions. Many English people wanted to fight Spain over this, but others felt it was not worth a war. However, when Captain Jenkins showed what looked like his cut-off ear to the British Parliament in 1738, it tipped the scale to the war side. In fall of 1739, England began fighting the "War of Jenkins' Ear" against Spain.

Some of the fighting had nothing to do with Georgia or Georgians. In late 1739, British naval forces captured a Spanish fort along Panama's northern coast. Two years later, British naval forces failed to capture Cartagena, along Colombia's northern coast.

The fighting between England and Spain very much involved Georgia and its people. There were two reasons for this. The Spanish thought that a portion of Georgia should belong to them. And

Georgia was the colony that was closest to Spanish possessions.

James Oglethorpe was placed in charge of English military forces in the Georgia region. Oglethorpe raised an army of Georgia colonists and friendly Indians, and sent out ships to guard Georgia's coast against a Spanish attack.

At the time, Georgia had an outpost of soldiers and their families on Amelia Island off Florida's far northeastern coast. In November of 1739, the Spanish killed two men on Amelia Island. Oglethorpe then decided it was time to attack the Spanish in Florida.

Between late 1739 and 1743, Oglethorpe's forces made several expeditions southward into Florida. They destroyed Spanish boats along the coast. In early 1740, Oglethorpe's forces seized two Spanish forts—Picolata and St. Francis— west of St. Augustine. Oglethorpe then planned to take St. Augustine, Spain's military headquarters in Florida and the oldest European-built city in what is now the United States.

Oglethorpe needed more men to attack St. Augustine. He asked South Carolina for men, but the older colony was less helpful than Oglethorpe had hoped. Nonetheless, by the spring of 1740, Oglethorpe had two thousand troops under his

Oglethorpe led an expedition against the Spanish in St. Augustine, Florida.

command. About half were colonial soldiers and half were friendly Indians—largely Cherokees, Creeks, and Yamacraws. Part of Oglethorpe's army went by water while the rest went by land to Florida.

As they approached St. Augustine, Oglethorpe's troops seized Fort San Diego and Fort Moosa. Oglethorpe hoped to overcome St. Augustine itself in an attack by land and sea. But Spanish ships protected St. Augustine by sea, so this plan was abandoned. Instead, Oglethorpe decided to keep his forces ringed around St. Augustine and starve out the enemy.

This proved to be disastrous to Oglethorpe's forces. Many of Oglethorpe's men came down with fevers. Not only that, but Spanish ships slipped through the British blockade and brought food to St. Augustine. After trying to starve out the Spaniards for thirty-eight days, Oglethorpe ended his siege in July of 1740 and brought his troops back to Frederica, Georgia. People called Oglethorpe's attack on St. Augustine a dismal failure. But by going on the attack, Oglethorpe may have kept the Spanish from invading Georgia—at least for a while.

The dreaded Spanish invasion came two years later, in 1742. In summer of that year, a large Spanish fleet sailed north from Cuba, stopping off at St. Augustine. By the time the fleet continued northward, it consisted of about fifty ships holding about four thousand soldiers and sailors. Their orders were to destroy towns and farms in

Oglethorpe planned to attack
by land and by sea.

Georgia and the Carolinas. These colonies—
especially Georgia—were now in danger of being
taken over by Spain.

James Oglethorpe gathered all available soldiers
and friendly Indians to protect England's southern American colonies. At first the Spanish did
well. They drove Oglethorpe's forces out of Fort St.
Simon on Georgia's St. Simons Island in late June
of 1742. But on July 7, when the Spanish tried to
seize Frederica on St. Simons Island, Oglethorpe's
troops drove them back. While retreating from
Frederica, the Spanish stopped to rest in a
marshy area of St. Simons Island.

Oglethorpe's forces, who were lying in wait at
this marshy area, suddenly attacked. So many

73

Fierce fighting took place during the Battle of Bloody Marsh.

Spaniards were killed that the marsh was said to have turned red from their blood. About five hundred Spanish soldiers were killed, wounded, or taken prisoner at this Battle of Bloody Marsh, which was fought on July 7, 1742.

Bloody Marsh is considered one of history's most important battles, for it ended the Spanish threat to Georgia and the Carolinas. A few days after their terrible loss, the Spanish left the Georgia region. Less than a year later, in the spring of 1743, Oglethorpe made one last try to seize St. Augustine. Again he failed. The "War of Jenkins' Ear" ended as a standoff. The English still had Georgia, and the Spanish still held Florida.

## OGLETHORPE LEAVES GEORGIA FOR GOOD

A few weeks after trying to seize St. Augustine that last time in 1743, James Oglethorpe returned to England. He had spent so much of his own money on Georgia that he badly needed funds himself, and he hoped the British government would repay him. Oglethorpe was also under personal attack in England. Not only did some people blame him for not capturing St. Augustine, an English soldier who had fought for him claimed that Oglethorpe had acted improperly as military commander. After reaching England, Oglethorpe was cleared of any wrongdoing as a military leader, and he was repaid the money he had spent on Georgia.

James Oglethorpe in a suit of armor

By the time Oglethorpe left Georgia in July of 1743, the colony was much different than had been planned. Georgia had been intended as a refuge mainly for poorer people. But out of the colonial population of about 2,500, only about half had been "charity" cases sent over at the Trustees' expense. The other half were "adventurers," some of whom were becoming wealthy and building large plantations. Instead of producing large amounts of wine and silk, the people raised cattle and were starting to grow such crops as rice, peaches, and tobacco.

Georgia's laws had undergone changes, too. By 1743, rum was allowed in Georgia. And by then Georgians could own up to several thousand rather than just five hundred acres of land. The plantation owners would not rest, however, until something else became legal.

Again and again the plantation owners asked the Trustees to allow slavery in Georgia. The Trustees finally repealed the ban on slavery in 1750. This had two results. Georgia joined the other twelve colonies in permitting the evil practice of human slavery. And the colony became more successful—as far as the white property owners were concerned.

Plantations were built on swampy land near the Savannah and Ogeechee rivers in eastern Georgia. Rice became the main crop that the slaves grew on these plantations, but they also grew other crops. Georgia's products were sold to England, to the British West Indies (islands off the coast of Florida), and to other colonies.

GEORGIA BECOMES A ROYAL COLONY

The Trustees had given Georgians more and more freedom in the 1740s and early 1750s. They has allowed Georgians to own slaves and larger pieces of land, and to buy and sell rum. One reason the Trustees were loosening their grip was that their authority was coming to an end. Back in 1732, King George II had granted the Trustees the right to operate Georgia for twenty-one years. After that, Georgia was to become a royal colony—one ruled by the king's own governors. Not long before they yielded control of the colony, the Trustees gave the people of Georgia a taste of self-government.

From the beginning, Georgians had been given no say in their own government. And from the beginning, many of them had complained about this. In 1751, the Trustees gave in to these complaints a bit—partly because of their fear that South Carolina would try to take over Georgia. By then, South Carolina had more than ten times Georgia's population—65,000 compared to the youngest colony's 6,000—and was much more powerful. The Trustees felt that if Georgians had some input in their government, they would do more to protect their colony.

In 1751, all the towns were allowed to send delegates to an Assembly in Savannah. This Assembly was not allowed to pass laws, but it could recommend laws that it wanted the Trustees to make for the colony. One of the Assembly's first recommendations was that emergency forces called militia be formed to defend the colony. The Trustees approved and the militia units were soon organized.

The Trustees had the right to run Georgia until the summer of 1753. But by the early 1750s, the Trustees had lost interest in the colony, and the English government was no longer giving them money to run Georgia. As a result, the Trustees gave up Georgia a year early, in June of 1752. Before handing Georgia over to George II, the Trustees obtained the king's promise that he would not let South Carolina seize the colony that had been named for him.

It took the king two years to set up the new royal government in Georgia. The people actually had more of a say in the new government than they had enjoyed under the Trustees. In overall charge of Georgia was a governor appointed by the king. Georgia's first royal governor was John Reynolds, who served from 1754 to 1757.

Georgia also now had a two-house legislative Assembly. The men in the Upper House were chosen by the king, while those in the lower, or Commons House, were elected by Georgia voters. The Commons House had less power than the

Upper House, however, because the king wanted to minimize the control Georgians had over their own affairs.

Although it was still one of the poorest of the Thirteen Colonies, Georgia grew more prosperous during its twenty-one years (1754-1775) as a royal colony. It wasn't the fact that the king now ruled Georgia directly that made the greatest difference. Slavery, which the Trustees had legalized in 1750, was the main factor. The rice and other crops that their slaves grew allowed more Georgians to become plantation owners. Between 1750 and 1760, Georgia's slave population grew from about one thousand to about four thousand people. During that time Georgia's overall population doubled from about 5,000 to about 10,000 people.

At Wormsloe Historic Site, visitors may tour the ruins of a house built in 1740 and watch demonstrations of colonial crafts.

# MARY MUSGROVE (1700?–1766?)

About fifty years after Tomochichi may have been born at Coweta, a baby girl was born there. Her father was a British trader about whom nothing is known. Her mother was a Creek Indian. The Creeks with whom she lived as a child called the little girl Cousaponakeesa.

When she was ten years old, Cousaponakeesa was taken to live among the English in South Carolina. She was baptized as a Christian by the English and sent to an English school.

In 1715-16, the Creeks joined the Yamassee Indians in fighting the South Carolina colonists. About the time the Yamassee War ended, Cousaponakeesa returned to Georgia to live with her mother's people. She had not been there long when a young man named John Musgrove arrived. The governor of South Carolina had sent John and his father to make peace with the Georgia Creeks. Cousaponakeesa and John Musgrove got married soon after they met. She then changed her name to Mary Musgrove—the name by which she is known to history.

John and Mary Musgrove lived among the Georgia Creeks for about seven years and then with the South Carolina colonists for nine more years. In 1732, the couple returned to Georgia and set up a trading post at Yamacraw Bluff. This was the spot where Tomochichi had settled with his followers a few years earlier, and where the first Georgia colonists settled. Mary Musgrove was the translator when Tomochichi and James Oglethorpe first met at Yamacraw Bluff in February of 1733.

Mary Musgrove proved to be very helpful to the Georgia colonists. Not only did she know both Creek and English, she was highly respected among the Indians. She and Oglethorpe became friends, and this helped cement relations between the colonists and the Indians. Mary Musgrove often translated when Oglethorpe spoke to Tomochichi or met with other Indians.

In the mid-1730s, Oglethorpe asked a big favor of Mary Musgrove. He asked her to open a trading post southwest of Savannah on the Altamaha River. He wanted her to keep track of Spanish activities for him. That way if the Spanish moved north to attack Savannah, she might be able to warn the colonists in time. Mary Musgrove agreed to this. She set up her Mount Venture trading post about one hundred miles southwest of Savannah about the time that her husband, John, died in 1735.

Mary Musgrove was especially helpful during the struggle between England and Spain known as the "War of Jenkins' Ear" (1739-1744). The Spanish wanted the Creeks to side with them, but Mary Musgrove helped convince them to stay loyal to the English.

Mary Musgrove performed another great service to Georgia that is rarely mentioned in history books. She sold the colonists meat, bread, and other foods that they needed in Georgia's early years. She expected to be paid for this food, but many of the colonists never paid what they owed her, so that she wound up supplying much of it for free.

While James Oglethorpe was in Georgia, Mary Musgrove was treated as a very important person. Oglethorpe liked her so much that when he left Georgia forever in 1743, he took a diamond ring from his finger and gave it to her. He also gave her a portion of the money that Georgia owed her for her services.

Once Oglethorpe left, relations between Mary Musgrove and the colonists fell apart. She was angry about the money she was still owed for helping the colonists in so many ways over the years. She was also insulted that she was no longer treated with respect. Mary Musgrove tried to force the colonists to give her more money, power, and land by turning the Indians against them. For a while, it even looked as if the Indians would attack Savannah under her orders. But the Georgia government squelched this threat by arresting Mary Musgrove and showing the Indians that they were ready to fight.

Finally, after many years of threatening and pleading, Mary Musgrove was paid a large sum of money and was given Georgia's St. Catherines Island. The woman who had done so much to help Georgia in its infancy retired there with her third husband. She died on St. Catherines Island.

---

# GEORGE WHITEFIELD (1714–1770)

George Whitefield was born in Gloucester, England. His parents ran the Bell Inn (a combination hotel-tavern) in Gloucester. When George was two years old, his father died. As soon as he was able, George began helping his mother at the inn. He poured drinks, cleaned rooms, and ran errands for her. He also went to school, where he showed great talent at giving speeches and acting.

George wanted to become an actor, but his mother considered acting a lowly job (like many other people of the time) and wouldn't let him. George had to be content with acting in school plays and watching the traveling actors who performed at the Bell Inn. This interest in drama helped him to later become one of history's most spellbinding preachers.

George's great-grandfather, great-great-grandfather, and several other relatives had been ministers. But young George was a pretty wild fellow who sometimes got drunk and did not seem cut out to become a preacher. However, when George was seventeen, his mother got him admitted to Oxford University. Shortly before George left for college, a Gloucester

George Whitefield preached throughout the colonies.

bookshop owner gave him a book entitled *A Serious Call to a Devout and Holy Life*. This book changed his life. George began to pray and sing psalms three times daily. He even went to church during the week.

George became even more devoted to religion at Oxford. There he met John and Charles Wesley, who led a Christian group (founded by Charles) called the "Holy Club." This group, which later grew into the Methodist Church, emphasized prayer, Bible study, and good deeds. George became one of the Holy Club's most devoted members. For his good deeds, he visited sick and poor people and prisoners and told them about God.

While at Oxford, George had several religious experiences. He underwent what he called a "new birth" that made him feel much closer to God. George decided to become a minister. In summer of 1736, he graduated from Oxford and was ordained.

That same summer, George gave his first sermon in his hometown of Gloucester. George spoke with such great feeling that some people fainted or went wild with excitement. Word spread that the twenty-two-year-old "Boy Preacher" had the power to help people feel the presence of God.

For the next several years, George Whitefield traveled and preached in various English cities and towns. He became a household name in England. Because of his belief that poor people who belonged to no church should have religion, he began preaching in fields and on street corners. Sometimes over 20,000 people gathered in a field to hear him.

George Whitefield's friends, the Wesley brothers, had gone to Georgia in 1735. Because so many adults had died during the first years of Georgia settlement, there were many orphans in the colony. George Whitefield decided to go to Georgia to help the orphans and preach to the Indians.

With several friends, he sailed from England in early 1738 and arrived in Savannah that May.

The Reverend Whitefield's first Georgia trip lasted just four months. During that time, he made plans to build an orphanage in Georgia. After returning to England in late 1738, he obtained, from the Georgia Trustees, a grant of five hundred acres. While preaching in England, he raised a great deal of money for his orphanage in Georgia.

Whitefield returned to America in late 1739. He preached to huge crowds in other colonies for several months, and then reached Georgia in early 1740. That year he began building the Bethesda Orphan House near Savannah. This orphanage contained one of Georgia's finest schools during colonial times. Still in existence, Bethesda is now the oldest orphanage in the United States.

In all, George Whitefield made seven voyages to America. Very few Europeans other than sailors visited colonial America as often. While in America he made many trips through the colonies, winning the hearts of thousands of poor people by preaching to them outdoors. He was a vital part of Colonial America's Great Awakening—a period of intense interest in religion that occurred during the 1700s.

Whitefield made a grand plan for Georgia. During the 1760s he tried to found Georgia's first college as part of the Bethesda Orphan House. But this plan fell through, and Georgia's first college (the University of Georgia) wasn't founded until 1785, after Whitefield's lifetime.

George Whitefield wore himself out preaching, but he would not listen when people told him to rest. "I had rather wear out than rust out," he said, on the last night of his life. This great preacher who meant so much to people on both sides of the Atlantic Ocean died in Massachusetts at the age of fifty-five.

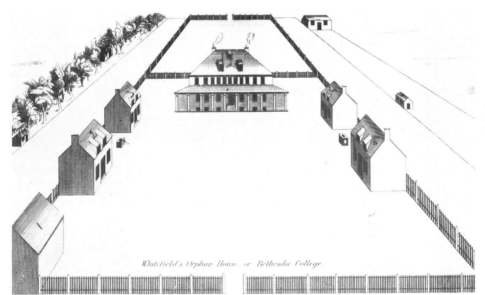

*Whitefield's Orphan House or Bethesda College.*

The Bethesda Orphan House was built in 1740.

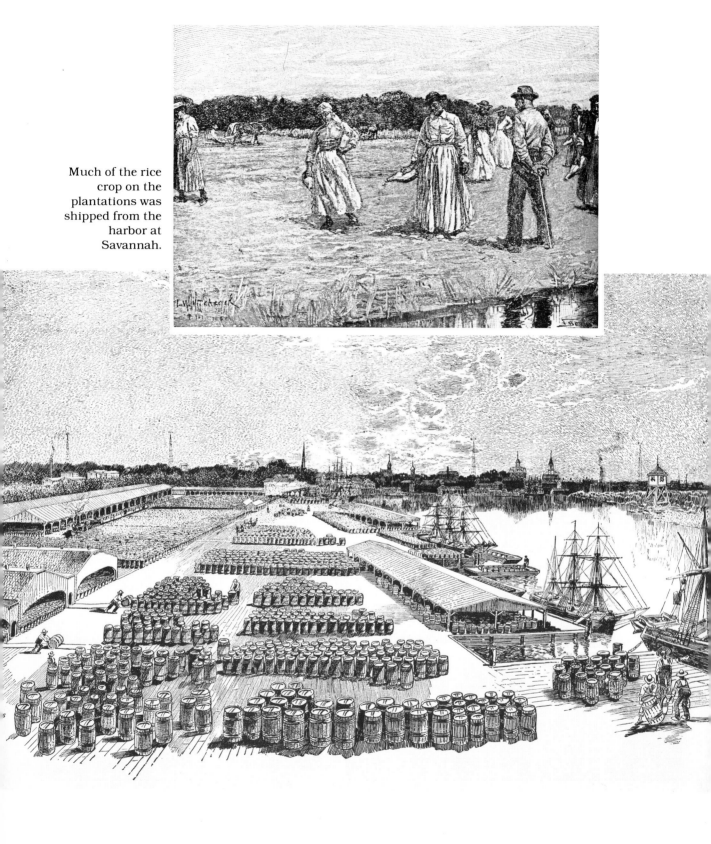

Much of the rice crop on the plantations was shipped from the harbor at Savannah.

# Chapter VI

## Life in Georgia During the Early 1760s

*Mix with two pounds flour half a pound of molasses, three-fourths ounce of caraways, one ounce of ginger finely sifted, and eight ounces of butter. After working it a great deal roll it and set it to rise.*

*Recipe for gingerbread from colonial Georgia*

### A COLONY OF FARMS AND SMALL TOWNS

By 1760, Georgia, the youngest of the Thirteen Colonies, was still a distant last in population with only about 10,000 non-Indians. Delaware, the colony with the next-smallest population, had about 33,000 people, while Virginia, the most populous colony, had about 340,000 people, or thirty-four times the number in Georgia!

If those 10,000 Georgians from the year 1760 could visit the state today, they would be amazed by what they'd see. Modern cities now stand in places that were just small towns or wilderness in 1760.

Georgia's five biggest cities today are Atlanta, Columbus, Savannah, Macon, and Albany in that order. Of those five, only Savannah even existed as of 1760. The other four, which are all located in the western half of the state, were not founded until the 1800s. As of 1760, no colonial town had been built in present-day central and western Georgia. Those regions were either empty or occupied by Indians.

In 1760, nearly all Georgia colonists lived on a strip of land about fifty miles wide along the Savannah River and the Atlantic Ocean. At that time, Savannah was Georgia's capital and main city. But Savannah was really just a small town compared to other colonial cities such as Philadelphia (Pennsylvania), Boston (Massachusetts), and New York City (New York).

Augusta and Darien were two other Georgia towns that existed both in 1760 and today. Back then, Georgia also had a number of little towns that no longer exist, including Sunbury, Frederica, Goshen, Bethany, Hampstead, and New Ebenezer.

Nearly all of the colonists who lived in Georgia in 1760 farmed. Even people who worked as lawyers, doctors, teachers, or merchants did a little farming. It was the rare family that did not produce at least some of its own food. By 1760, Georgia had three main types of farms. Most people lived on medium-sized farms. There were also many who lived on poor, often small farms. Only a few colonists owned large plantations.

More than half of Georgia's colonial families owned medium-sized farms where they grew corn and other crops and raised livestock. Some of these families had a slave or two to help with the farm work, but most of them owned no slaves. And some of these families produced more food than they needed and sold the excess to bring in money.

Colonial Georgia also had a surprising number of poor families—about thirty percent of the total white population. These people had no slaves, and struggled to grow enough food to feed themselves.

Pioneer farmer stands guard.

These poorest families lived mainly on what was then the frontier—the northern and western edges of the strip of land along the Savannah River and the Atlantic Ocean. Some of them had been "indentured servants." Their sea voyage to Georgia had been paid for by wealthy people. In return, they had to work as servants for about seven years. At the end of their period of service, the indentured servants had been released and given small pieces of land.

During the 1800s, when cotton was Georgia's main crop, the state had hundreds of plantations on which slaves did the work. But in the 1760s, when rice was still the main crop grown on

Slaves did all the hard work on the rice plantations.

Georgia's big farms, not very many plantations existed as yet. In fact, fewer than one out of every four families owned even a single slave.

## HOW THE COLONISTS BUILT THEIR HOUSES AND TOWNS

When a family moved to Georgia, its first task was building a home. In colonial times, nearly all of Georgia was forested. People cut down pines and other trees to clear space for their farms, then used the wood to build farmhouses.

Many frontier families built simple log cabins. Nearer the coast, people built a variety of wooden homes ranging from tiny huts to large homes. As late as 1762, Savannah had just three brick homes and about two hundred wooden houses. Many Georgians painted their homes blue, red, or white, which made the towns quite colorful. Churches and government buildings were usually made of wood, too.

This wooden house has a chimney made of tabby.

In Frederica and some other coastal towns, a building material called *tabby* was used. Tabby was made by mixing oyster shells, sand, and lime with water. Tabby was more durable than wood. Although few wooden buildings dating from colonial times still stand in Georgia, a number of tabby structures can still be seen.

Some rich Georgians bought furniture shipped from England, but many people's chairs, tables, and beds were made of Georgia wood, just like their houses. Only rich people had rugs on their floors in the 1760s. Many homes had nothing but sand on the floors.

### GEORGIA'S GREAT VARIETY OF PEOPLE

True, Georgia was the least-populous, the youngest, and one of the poorest of the Thirteen Colonies. But it also had a greater variety of people than nearly all of the other twelve colonies.

About two-thirds of all white Georgians were English. But Georgia in the 1760s had people who had come from Scotland, Ireland, Germany, France, Spain, Portugal, Switzerland, and Austria. These people had all gone to live in Georgia voluntarily. The colony was also home to people who had been sent to Georgia against their will. These were the slaves, many of whom had been taken from what are now the western African nations of Angola, Gambia, and Ghana. There were also some Indians living near Georgia's colonial towns.

In later years, most of these people's descendants learned English as their common language. But back in the 1760s, many of the colonists spoke the language of their "old country." Besides English, visitors to Georgia could hear people speaking Gaelic (a language of Ireland and Scotland), German, French, Spanish, and various African and Indian languages.

Because of its variety of people, the Georgia Colony had a variety of religions. Georgia was home to Lutherans, Presbyterians, Church of Englanders, Congregationalists, Jews, and people who followed the traditional African and Indian religions.

## DAILY LIFE

Daily life was very easy for some Georgians, and very difficult for others. The slaves had the worst life. According to laws passed in 1755, slaves could be made to work up to sixteen hours a day, six days a week. They were supposed to have Sunday off, but many masters ignored this rule and forced their slaves to work on that day too.

The slaves were given little clothing, and many of them had little to eat besides corn and rice. They were beaten if they broke certain plantation rules, and a slave who set a fire or attacked a white person could be executed. Slaves were forbidden to travel without written permission. Even when allowed off the plantation, a slave

Slaves unloading rice

could not mingle with other slaves unless a white person was present. The colonists feared that if slaves gathered together they might plan a revolt.

Masters were supposed to make sure that their slaves learned about Christianity. But a key part of the 1755 Slave Code was the law forbidding slaves from learning to read and write. The colonists did not want their slaves writing notes to each other or reading books about human rights.

Because the slaves were prevented from writing, we do not know their exact thoughts, but their actions show that they hated what was being done to them. Hundreds of Georgia slaves ran away, only to be captured in many cases. Some slaves even stole boats and rowed out to sea in hope of reaching Africa. They had been chained up during the Atlantic Ocean crossing and did not know how far America was from Africa.

Life was best for the plantation owners. By 1760, it was common for them to have a home in Savannah or another town in addition to their plantation. According to a joke of the time, ten in the morning was too early for a plantation owner to get out of bed. Slaves cooked and served the master and his family such tasty dishes as shrimp and oyster soups, stuffed fish, gingerbread, pecan

A planter's house in Georgia

cornsticks, and brandied cheesecake. The family traveled about by carriage, and their children frequently were educated by private tutors.

Most Georgians never tasted brandied cheesecake or slept until ten in the morning! Life for the majority of the Georgia colonists was composed of simple foods and plenty of hard work. Besides growing corn and other vegetables and raising cattle, most colonists hunted and fished. They made a variety of soups and stews, which they cooked in pots hung over the fireplace.

Most farmers lived in simple cabins.

These hardworking Georgians rode from place to place on horseback or on horse-pulled carts. As

Thatch-roofed schoolhouse in Georgia

for education, Georgia had no public school system as yet, and few families could afford tutors. However, some children attended the private schools that had been founded in Savannah, Augusta, and the other major towns. The farther out on the frontier a family lived, the less likely were their children to get any education at all.

It was common for colonial Georgians to have another job besides farming. When they weren't planting, caring for, or harvesting their crops, many Georgians worked as lawyers, doctors, carpenters, shoemakers, blacksmiths, merchants, cabinetmakers, and tailors. In the towns, some people had their shops right inside their homes.

NEWSPAPERS, BOOKS, AND ENTERTAINMENT

Like most people today, the Georgians of the 1760s wanted to know what was happening in the world. But in those days, it took ships several months to bring news from Europe to the

## T H E ROYAL
## Georgia Gazette.

SAVANNAH: THURSDAY, DECEMBER 9, 1779.     [N°. 41.]

American Colonies, and several weeks passed before news of an event in the Northern colonies reached the Southern ones. Because news traveled so slowly, the newspapers were constantly printing articles about events that had taken place weeks or even months earlier.

Making things worse for Georgians was the fact that, until 1763, they had no newspaper of their own. Georgians who were eager for news had to obtain papers from South Carolina or other colonies. The papers took days or weeks to get there, meaning that the news was even older by the time Georgians read about it.

The newspaper situation was improved for Georgians in April of 1763. That month, the Savannah bookseller and printer James Johnston founded the colony's first newspaper, the *Georgia Gazette*. The *Gazette* contained news articles, letters, essays, advertisements, and even poems.

In those days, relatively few copies of each newspaper were printed. The papers were passed from person to person, much like paperback books today. Georgians who did not know how to read sat in taverns and inns and listened as educated people read the news aloud.

The *Gazette* was founded at a time when many important events were taking place in Georgia and in the other colonies. In 1763, the war that England and France had fought over North American lands ended. The English were victorious in this last French and Indian War. Although no fighting had taken place in Georgia, the English victory meant a great deal to the colony. According to a complex peace treaty, Spain's Florida territory passed into English hands, making Georgia safe from Spanish attacks from Florida.

Also in 1763, Georgia's royal governor, James Wright, made a deal with the Indians. The Indians granted the colonists about five thousand square miles of eastern Georgia land. This paved the way for more settlers to come to Georgia and for the colony to start spreading out from the ocean and the Savannah River. Wright's agreement with the Indians—and measures taken by a previous royal governor, Henry Ellis—helped Georgia more than double its population (from 10,000 to 23,000) between 1760 and 1770.

Books were very expensive in colonial days compared to today. Many Georgians owned just a single book—the Bible. If a family owned fifteen books, that was considered a big private library.

Button Gwinnett, who later signed the Declaration of Independence for Georgia, owned about twenty books. Among the most popular books were ones on religion and law. Also popular were almanacs—books that gave the times of sunrises and sunsets for the coming year, predicted the weather, and advised the best times for planting. The first almanac printed in Georgia was probably *Tobler's Almanack*. James Johnston, the founder of Georgia's first newspaper, began printing *Tobler's Almanack* in 1764. Educated Georgians also liked to read such racy novels of the time as *Tom Jones* and *Fanny Hill*.

Because books were rather rare, Georgians founded libraries so that people could share reading materials. By the early 1760s, Georgia had at least five good libraries—three in Savannah, one in New Ebenezer, and one in Augusta. This growing interest in newspapers and books was taking place among people in all Thirteen Colonies in the mid-1700s, and helped inspire the Revolutionary War. As people read books about human rights, they began to think they deserved more rights from England. And as they read the news from the other colonies, they began to think of Americans as belonging to one nation.

Button Gwinnett

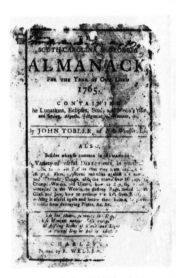

Copy of the 1765 edition of *Tobler's Almanack*

Georgians had livelier ways than reading to entertain themselves. Many people have the wrong idea that the colonists were all "goody-goodies." In fact, the colonists were for the most part a hard-living, daring bunch of people who had risked their lives in coming to a new country. They probably drank more liquor, gambled more, and got into more trouble than Americans today.

There was a widespread belief in colonial days that water was unhealthy. That was one reason for the great popularity of alcoholic drinks in colonial America. It was even common for children to drink beer or alcoholic cider instead of water.

Taverns and inns were favorite meeting places.

Perhaps because the water from its swamplands was especially unhealthy, Georgia was one of the hardest-drinking colonies of all. It was estimated that, in the 1760s, seventy percent of the white adults in Georgia drank an average of about half a pint of rum a day. The rum, combined with the wine, beer, rye whiskey, and peach and apple brandy that were also popular, kept a good portion of the population drunk much of the time. The *Georgia Gazette* printed articles against drunkenness and ministers preached against it, but people went right on drinking.

Games and sports were important forms of recreation with the men. Many men spent their evenings in the taverns gambling at cards, dice, billiards, and backgammon. Sometimes men who owned fast horses would race them over a level stretch of ground while the crowd bet on the race's outcome. Cricket, skittles (a forerunner of bowling), quoits (a game like horseshoes), and a sport that was a forerunner of football were also popular in colonial Georgia.

Spinning wheels were used to spin wool into yarn.

Women were excluded from playing at games and sports and gambling in Georgia's taverns, just as they were in the other colonies. Women were expected to stay home and cook, sew clothes, and care for the children. Among the few forms of entertainment that included women were dances, balls, concerts, and visiting with friends.

## PREJUDICE AND POLITICS IN COLONIAL GEORGIA

Unfortunately, some Americans today hate people simply because of their religion or color. There was plenty of prejudice in colonial times, too. The difference is that today the United States has laws to protect people from being harmed by prejudice. For example, all Americans now have the legal right to worship as they please and live where they want. But in the 1600s and 1700s, what we would call prejudice was built right into some of the laws of the Thirteen Colonies.

Georgia was more accepting of Jewish people than most of the other colonies, but there was widespread prejudice against Catholics in Georgia. In fact, Catholics were banned from the colony. One reason Georgians disliked Catholics was that England's two main enemies—Spain and France—were Catholic countries.

Another aspect of religion in Georgia that was unfair by modern standards was that the colony had an official faith. The Church of England had been made Georgia's official religion in 1758. This did not mean that everyone had to belong to the

Church of England. But all Georgia taxpayers—no matter what their religion—had to pay taxes to support the Church of England.

Of all the people in Georgia, the blacks suffered most from prejudice. The women and poor whites also suffered from prejudice. These three groups received little or no education. There were also laws to make sure that they were excluded from politics, just as they were in the other colonies.

Men owning at least fifty acres of land were the only ones who could vote for the Assembly. To serve in the Assembly, a man had to own five hundred acres of land. This left out the blacks, the poor whites, and all women. The idea that poorer farmers and shopkeepers had the right to vote and serve in government was something that only began to develop at the end of colonial times, when Americans began to break away from England.

The land was cleared by hand.

# HENRY ELLIS (1721–1806)

Born in Ireland, Henry Ellis studied to become a lawyer, but discovered that he had more interest in science than in law. Throughout his life, Ellis had a burning desire to learn all he could about scientific subjects such as weather, the oceans, the way the earth works, and plants and animals.

During the 1700s, Europeans wanted to find a "Northwest Passage" through North America. This was a waterway thought to connect the Atlantic to the Pacific Ocean. If such a waterway existed, ships from Europe could sail through it all the way to Japan, China, and other Asian lands. That would be much easier than sailing around Africa to get to Asia.

The English began looking for the Northwest Passage during the late 1500s. Over the next two centuries, they sent out ships that explored Hudson Bay and other bodies of water in Canada. The ships followed one route after another on these explorations, only to run up against land every time before reaching the Pacific Ocean.

By the 1740s, the British government offered a huge reward for the first expedition to find the Northwest Passage. One group in England planned to send out two ships—the *Dobbs Galley* and the *California*—to search for it in 1746. The expedition's planners wanted a scientist on board. Four days before the ships were to depart, Henry Ellis happened to return to England from Italy. Ellis was hired as the expedition's scientist.

The two ships left England in mid-1746, with Henry Ellis aboard the *Dobbs Galley*. The ships sailed north and west and in several weeks reached the region of icebergs around Greenland. Upon reaching Canada, the ships sailed into Hudson Bay and spent several months searching for the Northwest Passage.

Henry Ellis and his shipmates faced many dangers. Once the two ships nearly crashed onto rocks in the fog. Another time, an Eskimo saved a smaller boat belonging to the expedition from smashing on sandbars. The expedition also spent a freezing winter in Canada during which several men died.

Ellis kept a journal of this expedition. In it he described the Eskimos and Indians they met, the places they saw, and the plants and animals of the far north. After failing to find the Northwest Passage (it wasn't found for more than a century, far to the north of Hudson Bay), the two ships returned to England in October of 1747.

In 1748, Ellis published a book based on his notes called *A Voyage to Hudson's-Bay, by the* Dobbs Galley *and* California, *in the Years 1746 and 1747, for Discovering a North West Passage*. Although rarely read today, it is an action-packed and fascinating book. It also reveals Ellis's kindness. He very much liked the Indians and Eskimos, and was upset that some English traders in Canada mistreated them.

Ellis became famous for this book, and for a second one he wrote on the search for the Northwest Passage two years later. Then, in 1756, a dramatic change took place in Henry Ellis's life. He was appointed royal governor of Georgia.

Henry Ellis arrived in Savannah in February of 1757. He replaced John Reynolds who had become very unpopular by acting too bossy and playing favorites. During his nearly four years in Georgia, Henry Ellis earned the respect of the Georgia colonists.

Ellis had three main goals for the young colony. He thought it should be made safer from attack, have greater population growth, and become wealthier. He worked especially hard on Georgia's defense. He met with large numbers of Indians and made a peace treaty with the Creeks in 1758. He built a number of forts to defend Georgia. He even paid for a gunboat out of his own pocket to defend Georgia's coast. And he settled the dispute between Mary Musgrove and the Georgia government.

Governor Ellis also had a plan to increase Georgia's population. He invited poor people from other colonies to move to Georgia. What made this unusual was that in colonial times most government leaders tried to make up ways to get rid of their poor people. Ellis also increased taxes to provide more money for the government, and made sure that more paper money was available to Georgia colonists.

Personally, Henry Ellis became known as a "character" around Savannah. He walked the streets of the Georgia capital with a thermometer tied to his umbrella. He wanted to check the outdoor temperatures as part of his scientific research.

The great popularity of both Henry Ellis and Georgia's third and final royal governor, James Wright, helped maintain the people's loyalty to England. It was partly because of these two well-liked governors that Georgians were so slow to join the revolutionary cause. Henry Ellis left Georgia in late 1760 because of poor health. He lived for nearly another half century, though, and continued his scientific research. He was doing ocean research at Naples, Italy, when he died at the age of eighty-four.

Portraits of the men who signed the Declaration of Independence

# Chapter VII

# The Revolutionary War

*Come and take it!*

> *Answer of Georgia patriot John McIntosh,*
> *when the British demanded that the*
> *Americans surrender a fort in Georgia*

England's victory in the French and Indian War in 1763 set off a chain of events that affected all Thirteen Colonies—even ones like Georgia where no fighting had occurred. According to the 1763 peace treaty, France turned Canada and all its American possessions east of the Mississippi River (except New Orleans) over to England. This meant that the colonists no longer had to fear French invasions. And the Indians, many of whom had fought on the French side, had been pushed westward. This opened the way for the steady move inland by the colonists that over the next century took them all the way to the west coast.

But the end of the French and Indian War also meant something else to the colonists—increased taxation. England faced a problem. How could it pay for all its expenses from the French and

Indian War? How could it pay for all the troops it needed to patrol American lands? The English Parliament in London came up with a solution. Americans had gained from the defeat of the French and the Indians, English lawmakers reasoned. So the Americans should pay new taxes to help provide money for the mother country.

Some English lawmakers realized that the Americans would hate these taxes. They warned the pro-taxation people that it might even result in war between the colonies and England. But the people who favored taxation won out, and between 1764 and 1773 England passed one tax law after another. The Americans were supposed to pay taxes on many items ranging from paper and paint to tea and sugar.

British tax stamp

One of the first of these tax laws—and one that enraged many colonists—was the Stamp Act. It ordered the colonists to buy special tax stamps and place them on legal papers such as wills and marriage licenses and also on their newspapers. Passed in the spring of 1765, the Stamp Act was to take effect on November 1, 1765. In the months before November 1, many Americans complained bitterly about the Stamp Act. Some people gave speeches and wrote letters to newspapers and

English officials in which they said "Taxation without representation is tyranny." They felt that the English government had no right to tax them because Americans were not allowed to serve in the Parliament.

In some places the Americans demonstrated and even rioted. Throughout the colonies, groups calling themselves "Sons of Liberty" or "Liberty Boys" formed. These men had a tendency to react violently, and later many of them served as soldiers when the Revolutionary War broke out. In Boston, the Sons of Liberty smashed buildings owned by British officials.

Georgia was home to some Sons of Liberty, too. In October of 1765, just a few days before the Stamp Act was to take effect, people in Savannah gathered to celebrate the fifth anniversary of George III's rule as king of Great Britain. Suddenly, Savannah's Sons of Liberty paraded out dummies dressed like a British tax officer and other British officials. The dummies were burned as a symbol of what the Sons of Liberty thought of the Stamp Act. However, most Georgians felt about the Stamp Act the way most Americans feel today when they hear about a tax increase. They opposed it, but they were not fighting mad.

To protest the tax stamp, the colonists burned dummies dressed like tax collectors in the public squares.

In October of 1765, the American colonists held a Stamp Act Congress in New York City to discuss how to deal with the crisis. Nine of the thirteen colonies were represented at this meeting. This was important because it showed that the colonies were starting to work together. Georgia was one of the four colonies that did not send delegates to the Stamp Act Congress. Georgia's Royal Governor James Wright talked the colony's Assembly out of sending representatives. Georgia was also the only colony that allowed tax stamps to be sold within its borders—although not many of them were sold there. However, when English lawmakers saw that the Stamp Act was causing so much trouble in so many of the colonies, they repealed it in early 1766.

Nonetheless, England passed more tax laws over the next few years. And for the most part, Georgia opposed these laws less violently than the other colonies. For example, in 1733, Parliament passed the Tea Act. To protest this tax, in December of 1773, patriots in Boston, Massachusetts, boarded three English ships and threw more than three hundred chests of tea they were holding into Boston Harbor. This defiant act became known as the "Boston Tea Party." A few months later, New York City patriots held a "tea party" by dumping British tea into the water. Patriots in Maryland and New Jersey burned British tea. Many Georgians, including lawmakers, opposed the Tea Act, but not with the spirit displayed in other colonies. In fact, during the troubles with England, Georgia had the highest percentage of people who sided with the mother country of all thirteen colonies. These people were called "Loyalists."

Georgians had reasons to be more loyal to England than the people in the other colonies. As of 1773, the other colonies were all over one hundred years old. Many families in those colonies had lived in America for at least five generations. These families no longer thought of themselves as English people who happened to live far from home. They thought of themselves as Americans. Most of them had never been to England, and knew about it only from reading about the mother country or by hearing stories from other people.

Georgia, on the other hand, was just forty years old in 1773. Many of its middle-aged and older people had been born in England, and still thought of themselves as transplanted Englishmen and Englishwomen. Also, one of the things the Trustees had considered when picking the first Georgia colonists was their loyalty to England. Only those who had seemed loyal to the mother country had been chosen.

In addition, Georgia had never been more prosperous than it was in the early 1770s. Georgians were selling rice, lumber, beef, and other products to Britain, to other European nations, and to the West Indies. Georgians were even having trouble meeting all the demands for their products. To cap things off, Georgians for the most part liked James Wright, who had replaced Henry Ellis as royal governor in 1760.

In the fall of 1774, American patriots held a big meeting in Philadelphia, Pennsylvania, to discuss all the troubles with the mother country. Each colony was asked to send delegates to this First Continental Congress, and twelve of the colonies did so. Georgians debated what to do, but in the end chose not to send anyone. Georgia was the only colony not represented in the Congress. People in other colonies began to wonder which side Georgia would support if war broke out between Britain and America.

Gradually, though, more and more Georgians were coming out on the side of the American patriots. This was especially true among the younger people, who in many cases opposed their parents on this issue. Among the leading Georgia patriots were Archibald Bulloch, John Houstoun, George Walton, Noble Wymberly Jones, and Button Gwinnett.

Headquarters for the patriots in Savannah was Tondee's Tavern, built by Peter Tondee in 1766 or 1767 on the corner of Broughton and Whitaker streets. Many patriotic speeches were made in Tondee's, and plans to involve Georgia more on the patriot side were hatched there.

War between the colonists and the English broke out on April 9, 1775. It began in Massachusetts, a thousand miles northeast of Georgia. At dawn on that April Wednesday, some British troops marched into the town of Lexington. Warned of the British approach by Paul Revere, Lexington's "minutemen" (militiamen) were waiting on the village green for them.

The British troops, called redcoats because of the color of their uniforms, may have smiled when they saw the Lexington minutemen. The Americans were not professional soldiers, but were really just a bunch of fathers, grandfathers, and teenaged boys standing there with their old guns. Someone fired a shot—from which side is not known—and the Battle of Lexington began. The Americans were badly beaten in this first battle of the Revolutionary War. Eight of their men were killed and ten were wounded, while the British had just one soldier wounded.

Across the Massachusetts countryside, Americans heard what had happened to their friends and neighbors at Lexington. Later that same day, the two sides faced each other again in nearby

Battle of Lexington

Concord, Massachusetts. This time the Americans
had more men than the British. They outfought
the redcoats at Concord, and then chased them
back to Boston. Nearly three hundred redcoats
were killed or wounded in this running Battle of
Concord, which was the Americans' first victory
in the Revolutionary War. The Americans had
about one hundred casualties.

As word spread that war with Britain had
begun, American patriots in all the colonies began

to rebel against the mother country. In Savannah, Georgia, the Sons of Liberty seized military supplies belonging to the king. These supplies were later used against the British in battles. The Georgians also sent rice and money up to the Boston region, where the Americans were gathering a large army.

Three weeks after the Battles of Lexington and Concord took place, the Second Continental Congress opened in Philadelphia. When it opened on May 10, 1775, Georgia again was not represented. Many Georgians still favored the British side, and the colony as a whole was not yet ready to commit itself to the American cause. However, one delegate from Georgia appeared in Philadelphia on May 13. He was Lyman Hall, of Midway, Georgia. Hall represented the Midway region only, and was not an official Georgia delegate.

The delegates attending the Second Continental Congress were enraged at Georgia. Congress even took steps to punish the youngest colony for not sending any official delegates. But even without this prodding, Georgia would have soon sent delegates to the Second Continental Congress. In July of 1775, an important meeting was held at Tondee's Tavern in Savannah. At this meeting, four men besides Lyman Hall were elected to be Georgia's first representatives at the Second Continental Congress. They were Archibald Bulloch, John Houstoun, Noble Wymberley Jones, and the Reverend John J. Zubly, all of Savannah.

Once in Philadelphia, the Georgia delegates helped the representatives from the other colonies direct the fighting of the war. In 1775, the Continental Congress organized the Continental Army, elected the Virginian George Washington to lead it, and told the colonies to start turning themselves into states.

James Wright

In Georgia, the people who supported American independence took complete control of the government and began to organize a new state government in 1775. Then, in early 1776, Georgia patriots arrested Royal Governor James Wright, who was still popular among many people but who was viewed by many others as a symbol of British power. After promising that he would not try to escape, Wright was allowed to remain in the governor's house. However, rowdy patriots frequently gathered in front of his home and threw stones as they called out insults. In February of 1776, the governor escaped and made his way to a British ship.

A month after Governor Wright fled, several English warships sailed up the river to Savannah and tried to seize eleven American ships. The American vessels carried rice, which the British wanted to feed their troops. A skirmish broke out between British and American forces at Savannah. Several men were killed and several others were wounded as the two sides exchanged gunfire. The British captured about 1,600 barrels of rice in this raid, but the Americans prevented them from getting more by burning several ships. Fought in early March of 1776, this minor skirmish known as the Battle of the Rice Boats was the first fight of the Revolutionary War to take place in Georgia.

The spring and summer of 1776 were crucial times for Americans in Georgia and at the Continental Congress in Philadelphia. Up in Pennsylvania's capital, Congress was discussing an important issue. Some delegates hoped that the colonies would gain more rights by fighting the war but would eventually return to British rule. Others wanted the Thirteen Colonies to separate from Britain and form a new country— the United States of America.

The new government Georgians had formed in 1775—the Georgia Provincial Congress—issued

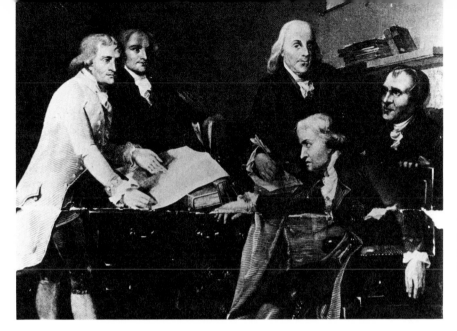

Thomas Jefferson, standing at left, wrote the Declaration of Independence.

orders to their delegates in Philadelphia in April of 1776. When it came to a vote, the delegates were to side with American independence. There were still many Georgians who favored British rule, but these people had little say in Georgia's new government. Also in April of 1776, the Georgia Provincial Congress issued a new constitution (set of basic laws) for Georgia, transforming it from a colony into a state.

On July 2, 1776, the Continental Congress voted on the independence issue. Twelve colonies, including Georgia, voted for independence. New York was the one holdout and did not vote that day, but it approved independence a few days later. Even before the July 2 vote, the Virginian Thomas Jefferson had written a paper explaining why the United States sought independence.

Button Gwinnett (left), George Walton (center), and Lyman Hall (right) signed the Declaration of Independence for the Georgia Colony.

Congress had wanted this document ready in case the delegates voted for independence. Called the Declaration of Independence, this paper was approved by the Continental Congress on July 4, 1776. Ever since, the Fourth of July has been celebrated as the birthday of the United States.

Three men signed the Declaration of Independence for Georgia. They were Georgia's Continental Congress delegates Button Gwinnett, Lyman Hall, and George Walton. Their signatures are on the far left side of the Declaration of Independence.

Copies of the Declaration were sent to the thirteen new states, where they were read to crowds in town after town. In Savannah, the Declaration was read aloud in Tondee's Tavern, along the riverbanks, and in many other places. Thirteen cannons were fired in Savannah to honor the thirteen new states. Throughout the colonies, people drank thirteen toasts.

Because it proclaimed that the United States was free of Britain, the Declaration of Independence has been called the nation's "birth certificate." At first, though, it looked like the newborn country would not live long. The United States disorganized army appeared to have little chance against Britain, which was the world's strongest nation.

The Continental Congress lacked the money to fight the war properly. As a result, the American soldiers were poorly trained, poorly clothed, poorly fed, poorly paid, and poorly armed. George Washington and his officers had trouble disciplining the men. Some left the army and went home when it was time to plant or harvest the crops. Before big battles, men ran away from the army by the hundreds.

Although his army was clearly losing to the British in the war's first years, George Washington kept American hopes alive. He did it by fighting small rather than big battles. Washington wanted to attack the British, but he knew that a major loss might end American chances for victory.

The low point for the American army was the winter of 1777-78. In December, Washington and his 11,000 men went into winter quarters at Valley Forge, Pennsylvania. The British could have destroyed the cold and sick army at Valley Forge, but smashing such a helpless foe would have looked bad to the world. Disease, hunger, and cold almost did the job for the redcoats anyway, for during that awful winter more than a fourth of Washington's men died at Valley Forge. Were it not for George Washington, the survivors might have given up. The man who became known as "the Father of His Country" had convinced his remaining troops that they could one day win, and he drilled them to make that a possibility.

In the spring of 1778, things began to look up for the Americans when France agreed to help them fight Britain. French soldiers, sailors, weapons, ships, and money eventually helped the Americans turn the tide and win the war, but for several more years it appeared that the British would still be victorious.

## THE WAR COMES TO GEORGIA

During the Revolutionary War's early years, British Loyalists from Florida known as *Florida Rangers* made raids into Georgia. The Florida Rangers stole cattle and attacked outlying settlements. Also during those years, American soldiers, many of them Georgians, tried three times to seize British-held St. Augustine, Florida. All three expeditions failed. Despite these events, Georgia and the rest of the South was, for the most part, untouched by fighting during the Revolution's early years.

In 1778, the British turned their attention to Georgia and made a plan. A large force would sail down from British-held New York. Another large British force would head north from Florida. The two armies would meet in Georgia and seize Savannah and other nearby regions.

By November of 1778, part of the British forces had reached Georgia. When the British tried to seize the town of Sunbury, an incident occurred that became legandary among Georgians. Fort

Morris, which protected Sunbury, was under the command of Georgia's Colonel John McIntosh. The British demanded that Colonel McIntosh surrender the fort. McIntosh sent back a challenge that Georgia patriots loved: "COME AND TAKE IT!" The British backed down on this occasion, although they did seize the fort a short time later.

Meanwhile, thousands of redcoats were pouring into Georgia. In late December of 1778, the British landed several thousand men near Savannah, which was defended by only several hundred patriots. The Americans tried to hold the town, but were overwhelmed. In a battle with the redcoats near Savannah, about one hundred Americans were killed or drowned in the swamps while trying to flee. Over four hundred patriots were captured. The British had only about twenty-five men killed or wounded.

Shortly after the British captured Savannah, the Americans won a big battle in Georgia. A British army of almost one thousand men marched into northern Georgia, where they destroyed farms and settlements. On February 14, 1779, they stopped to rest at a place called Kettle Creek in Georgia's Wilkes County. A large American force made up mainly of men from the Carolinas and Georgia attacked the British at

Kettle Creek on that Valentine's Day. About one hundred and fifty British soldiers were killed, wounded, or captured. Only about thirty American men were killed or wounded during their victory at the Battle of Kettle Creek.

Despite this American victory, the British were seizing town after town in Georgia. In July of 1779, James Wright returned to Savannah and reestablished royal rule over Georgia. Hundreds of families that had remained loyal to the English celebrated. They were well treated by the British and hundreds of their men joined the king's army.

The American and French leaders knew that winning back Savannah was a key to winning back all of Georgia, and to keeping other important Southern cities from falling into British hands. In 1779, the French and American forces tried to retake Savannah.

In September of that year, a French fleet of twenty-two ships under Count Jean Baptiste Charles Henri Hector d'Estaing arrived at Savannah. Aboard the ships were four thousand French troops. Meanwhile, General Benjamin Lincoln, commander of the Continental Army in the South, approached Savannah with about two thousand men.

Count d'Estaing

American and French forces attacked the British forces defending Savannah on October 8, 1779.

It looked as if the British would have to give up Savannah against this large force. But the British commander at Savannah asked for a day to consider the matter. D'Estaing made the mistake of granting this request. During that time, the British obtained nearly one thousand more soldiers from South Carolina. The additional help enabled the British to defend Savannah instead of surrendering it.

Count d'Estaing then decided to bombard Savannah from a distance. The bombardment began on October 4 and continued for five days. Then, on October 9, the French and the American forces joined in a direct attack upon Savannah. This attack was one of the most terrible defeats for the Americans of the entire Revolutionary War.

During the hour and a half that the Battle of Savannah lasted, over one thousand French and American troops were killed or wounded. Among the dead was the famous Polish soldier Casimir Pulaski, who had joined the American side. Count d'Estaing was among the wounded. This awful defeat for the American and French forces at Savannah was a blow to South Carolina as well as Georgia. It enabled the British to capture South

Count Casimir Pulaski

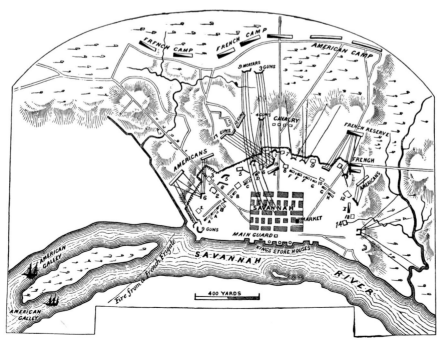

Plan of the attack on Savannah

Carolina's capital city of Charleston a few months later. By the spring of 1780, this British victory also helped the British extend their control over all of Georgia except a small area not far from Augusta.

Hundreds of patriotic Georgia families fled the state during those dark days. Many families that wanted to stay were kicked out by British troops, who lived in their homes and often ransacked them. Some Georgians who continued to fight the British in skirmishes were captured and executed. Nonetheless, in 1780 and 1781, brave bands of Georgians continued to make small attacks on the British while praying for the return of a large American force.

The Georgia patriot Robert Sallette was one of those who went on fighting the British with a small band of men. According to one unproven story, a wealthy Loyalist offered a large reward for the head of Sallette, whom he had never seen. Sallette decided to collect the reward himself. He dressed up as a farmer, packed a pumpkin into a sack, and visited the Loyalist.

Sallette told the man that he had Robert Sallette's head with him. The Loyalist asked to see it, but Sallette refused to open the sack unless he got the reward first. Once he had the money, Sallette took off his hat, pointed to his head, and said, "Here is Sallette's head!" It was reported that Sallette then shot the Loyalist.

Nancy Hart was another Georgian whose cleverness and bravery became legendary. Nancy and her husband, Captain Benjamin Hart, lived with their children on Georgia's northeastern frontier. Many people in that region had fled to safer areas, but the Harts had refused to leave their home. One day in 1780, about half a dozen Loyalists stopped at the Hart cabin when the captain was away. It was believed that these men had murdered the patriot leader John Dooly at his home near Augusta, Georgia, a short time earlier.

The Loyalists ordered Nancy Hart to cook them a meal. While she cooked, Mrs. Hart sent her daughter Sukey out—supposedly to fetch water. Sukey really summoned her father and some neighbors. Meanwhile, Nancy Hart took a big drink of corn liquor that one of the Loyalists offered her and acted friendly toward the men. She wanted them to think that they had nothing to fear from her.

As the Loyalists drank and Nancy cooked, she went from time to time to the corner of the cabin where the men had stacked their guns. She slipped several of the guns through a crack

Nancy Hart was one of the heroes of the American Revolution.

between the cabin logs. Suddenly, the Loyalists noticed what she was doing. When one of them moved toward her, Mrs. Hart shot and killed him with one of the guns. With another gun she wounded the next man who moved toward her. Captain Hart and his friends then appeared and took the Loyalists prisoner. It was said that Captain Hart wanted to shoot the Loyalists, but that Nancy Hart talked him out of it. She thought shooting was too good for them and convinced her husband and his friends to hang them!

Georgia patriots also bravely kept the state government going during the British occupation. Although James Wright had set up a royal government once more in Savannah, that government was illegal in the eyes of the Georgia patriots. They maintained their own government, but to avoid being captured by the British, it had to move around. From the spring of 1780 until July of 1781, it is not known where the state government was located. It may have been in Wilkes County, northwest of Augusta, part of the time, and across the Savannah River in South Carolina part of the time.

Events outside Georgia helped bring about the recapture of the state by American forces. By 1781, George Washington had been waiting six years to launch a big attack on the British. His chance finally came in October of 1781 when American and French forces gave the British a crushing defeat at Yorktown, Virginia. The Battle of Yorktown was the Revolution's pivotal battle, and resulted in the Americans winning the war.

By the end of 1781 though, the British still occupied Georgia. In early 1782, the American

"Mad Anthony" Wayne

General "Mad" Anthony Wayne was sent by George Washington to help drive the British out of Georgia. In June of 1782, Wayne defeated several hundred Indians who were fighting for the British in Georgia's last Revolutionary War battle. Seeing that their cause in Georgia and elsewhere in the colonies was lost, the British left Georgia in July of 1782 and Charleston, South Carolina, in December of 1782. Great Britain signed a peace treaty with the new country—the United States of America—in September of 1783. The Revolutionary War was over. Georgia and the other twelve states had freed themselves from Great Britain!

# BUTTON GWINNETT (1735?–1777)

Born in Gloucestershire, England, Button Gwinnett was the son of a minister. Gwinnett married at the age of twenty-two, and went into business as a merchant at about that time. As part of his business, he sold goods to the Thirteen American Colonies.

Button Gwinnett liked talking to the sailors and sea captains who carried his goods to the colonies. Their stories about America excited him. In about 1764, Button Gwinnett and his wife packed up and moved to Charleston, South Carolina, where they lived for a short while. By 1765, they had settled in Savannah, Georgia.

Button Gwinnett operated a general store in the Georgia capital. Advertisements for his goods can still be seen in the old copies of the *Georgia Gazette*. After living in Savannah for a while, the Gwinnetts decided to move away from town and become farmers. They bought Georgia's St. Catherines Island, where by the early 1770s, they were operating a plantation.

Although his home was on the island, Button Gwinnett spent a great deal of time on the mainland. He listened as people discussed the troubles with England during the 1770s. For a man who had been in America just ten years, the fiery and opinionated Gwinnett did something unusual. He put his heart and soul into the American cause and opposed the country of his birth. It was said that for a while Gwinnett had been undecided as to which side to take, and that Lyman Hall of Midway, Georgia, convinced Gwinnett of the rightness of the American cause.

In early 1776, Georgians elected Button Gwinnett as one of their representatives to the Continental Congress. He served just a few brief months in Congress—but these were the crucial months during which the new nation was born. Gwinnett was one of three Georgians (along with Lyman Hall and George Walton) to sign the Declaration of Independence.

Even though he was no military man, Button Gwinnett wanted to be made general of Georgia's troops. In this way he resembled Virginia's Patrick Henry, a great speaker who wanted to lead troops more than anything else. And just as Patrick Henry failed in his brief military career, so did Button Gwinnett. To start with, Lachlan McIntosh, a more experienced military man, was placed in charge of Georgia's troops. Gwinnett instead was elected speaker of the Georgia Assembly, where he helped create the state constitution of 1777.

In February of 1777, Archibald Bulloch, the state governor of Georgia who had replaced Royal Governor Wright, suddenly died. Button Gwinnett

Lachlan McIntosh

was named acting governor until an election later that year. He soon was feuding bitterly with the McIntosh family. He ordered the arrest of George McIntosh, who had been accused of being a traitor to the American cause. George was the brother of Lachlan, who had been placed in charge of Georgia troops, and of John, who later told the British to "Come and take it [the fort]!" Button Gwinnett also used his position as governor to take military power away from General Lachlan McIntosh.

In the spring of 1777, Governor Gwinnett planned an expedition to seize British-held Florida. He excluded General McIntosh from the planning, and led the expedition himself. This attempted attack failed, partly due to Gwinnett's treatment of General McIntosh. Because of this, Gwinnett lost the election for governor in May of 1777. But when the two men went before the Georgia Assembly to explain why the attack on Florida had failed, Gwinnett outtalked Lachlan McIntosh. Feeling that he was being blamed unfairly for the unsuccessful attack, McIntosh called Gwinnett "a scoundrel and a lying rascal" in front of Georgia lawmakers.

Button Gwinnett died as a result of his duel with Lachlan McIntosh.

Back in those days, men sometimes fought duels with pistols over such insults. Not a man to avoid a fight, Button Gwinnett challenged General McIntosh to a duel. The two men met on the outskirts of Savannah on a May morning in 1777. Holding their guns, they stood face to face about twelve feet apart.

At a signal, both men fired. Gwinnett was shot in the thigh and McIntosh in the leg. Incredibly, the two of them shook hands, having settled their dispute in what was considered a "gentlemanly" way.

Lachlan McIntosh recovered, but Button Gwinnett's wound became terribly infected. Even according to the poor medical standards of the time, Gwinnett seems to have been poorly treated by his doctor. Several days after the duel, Button Gwinnett died. Although Button Gwinnett had been one of the most dedicated patriots in Georgia, his fierce temper and spitefulness regarding Lachlan McIntosh had brought him an early death.

One interesting fact about Button Gwinnett concerns his signature. Because he signed the Declaration of Independence, and because there are only about thirty-six examples of his autograph in existence, Button Gwinnett's signature is extremely valuable. A signed Button Gwinnett document has sold for as much as $100,000!

*Button Gwinnett*

# We the People

George Washington, standing at right, was the president of the constitutional convention that wrote the Constitution of the United States of America.

# Chapter VIII

# The Fourth State

*Georgia [had in the 1770s and 1780s] one of the more democratic state governments, usually listed with Pennsylvania and North Carolina as being leaders in this regard.*

*From* Colonial Georgia: A History *by Kenneth Coleman*

Few Americans realize it today, but during the first years after the Revolutionary War it looked like the country would fall apart. The United States was governed by laws called the Articles of Confederation, which the thirteen states had approved in 1781. The problem was that the Articles granted little power to the Continental Congress, which still served as the central government. In most ways, each state government had more power than the federal government.

The country had no president to lead it, no federal courts, and no power to raise taxes. The Congress, which was often broke, had to beg the states for money. Most of the states refused to provide the funds. As a result, the United States could not afford more than a tiny army, and could not pay many of its debts.

Since the United States broke some of its promises to them, other countries lost respect for the new nation. There was great danger that a foreign power—perhaps even Britain or France— would try to conquer the United States. Some Americans thought that only the leadership of a king could save the young country.

To make matters worse, the states continually fought one another over money, borders, the use of rivers and ports, and other matters. The United States government was too weak to settle these disputes. There was even danger that one or more of the states would withdraw from the nation and form a separate country.

By 1787, most Americans saw that something had to be done about this situation. A national convention was held in Philadelphia between May and September of 1787 to reorganize the govern- ment. Every state but Rhode Island sent delegates to this Constitutional Convention.

By this time, Georgia had a very fine state constitution. Some historians say that Georgia, Pennsylvania, and North Carolina were the three states with the finest state constitutions during America's early years of independence. Georgia's constitution allowed more people to vote and take part in government than the constitutions of most of the other new states.

Georgians wanted the national government to be democratic and strong. Georgia sent four delegates to the Constitutional Convention—William Few, Abraham Baldwin, William Pierce, and William Houstoun. These men helped draft a democratic and strong set of national laws—the United States Constitution. William Few and Abraham Baldwin signed the Constitution for Georgia.

William Few

Under the rules of the new Constitution, each ex-colony would become a state when it ratified (approved) the document. Delaware became the first state by ratifying the new Constitution on December 7, 1787. Pennsylvania, followed by New Jersey, became the second and third states a few days later. On January 1, 1788, Georgia approved the Constitution. The land where Mound Builders and then Creek and Cherokee Indians had once lived, where Tomochichi had helped James Oglethorpe found a colony built on noble ideals, and where people like Nancy Hart and Robert Sallette had fought for liberty, thus became the fourth state to join the United States under the new Constitution!

Abraham Baldwin

# Colonial America Time Line

Before the arrival of Europeans, many millions of Indians belonging to dozens of tribes lived in North America (and also in Central and South America)

**About 982 A.D.**—Eric the Red, born in Norway, reaches Greenland during one of the first European voyages to North America

**About 985**—Eric the Red brings settlers from Iceland to Greenland

**About 1000**—Leif Ericson (Eric the Red's son) leads what is thought to be the first European expedition to mainland North America; Leif probably lands in Canada

**1492**—Christopher Columbus, sailing for Spain, reaches America

**1497**—John Cabot reaches Canada in the first English voyage to North America

**1513**—Ponce de León of Spain explores Florida

**1519-1521**—Hernando Cortés of Spain conquers Mexico

**1565**—St. Augustine, Florida, the first permanent European town in what is now the United States, is founded by the Spanish

**1607**—Jamestown, Virginia is founded, the first permanent English town in the present-day U.S.

**1608**—Frenchman Samuel de Champlain founds the village of Quebec, Canada

**1609**—Henry Hudson explores the eastern coast of present-day U.S. for The Netherlands; the Dutch then claim parts of New York, New Jersey, Delaware, and Connecticut and name the area New Netherland

**1619**—Virginia's House of Burgesses, America's first representative lawmaking body, is founded

**1619**—The first shipment of black slaves arrives in Jamestown

**1620**—English Pilgrims found Massachusetts' first permanent town at Plymouth

**1621**—Massachusetts Pilgrims and Indians hold the famous first Thanksgiving feast in colonial America

**1622**—Indians kill 347 settlers in Virginia

**1623**—Colonization of New Hampshire is begun by the English

**1624**—Colonization of present-day New York State is begun by the Dutch at Fort Orange (Albany)

**1625**—The Dutch start building New Amsterdam (now New York City)

**1630**—The town of Boston, Massachusetts is founded by the English Puritans

**1633**—Colonization of Connecticut is begun by the English

**1634**—Colonization of Maryland is begun by the English

**1635**—Boston Latin School, the colonies' first public school, is founded

**1636**—Harvard, the colonies' first college, is founded in Massachusetts

**1636**—Rhode Island colonization begins when Englishman Roger Williams founds Providence

**1638**—The colonies' first library is established at Harvard

**1638**—Delaware colonization begins when Swedish people build Fort Christina at present-day Wilmington

**1640**—Stephen Daye of Cambridge, Massachusetts prints *The Bay Psalm Book*, the first English-language book published in what is now the U.S.

**1643**—Swedish settlers begin colonizing Pennsylvania

**1647**—Massachusetts forms the first public school system in the colonies

**1650**—North Carolina is colonized by Virginia settlers in about this year

**1650**—Population of colonial U.S. is about 50,000

**1660**—New Jersey colonization is begun by the Dutch at present-day Jersey City

**1670**—South Carolina colonization is begun by the English near Charleston

**1673**—Jacques Marquette and Louis Jolliet explore the upper Mississippi River for France

**1675-76**—New England colonists beat Indians in King Philip's War

**1682**—Philadelphia, Pennsylvania is settled

**1682**—La Salle explores Mississippi River all the way to its mouth in Louisiana and claims the whole Mississippi Valley for France

**1693**—College of William and Mary is founded in Williamsburg, Virginia

**1700**—Colonial population is about 250,000

**1704**—*The Boston News-Letter*, the first successful newspaper in the colonies, is founded

**1706**—Benjamin Franklin is born in Boston

**1732**—George Washington, future first president of the United States, is born in Virginia

**1733**—English begin colonizing Georgia, their thirteenth colony in what is now the United States

**1735**—John Adams, future second president, is born in Massachusetts

1743—Thomas Jefferson, future third president, is born in Virginia

1750—Colonial population is about 1,200,000

1754—France and England begin fighting the French and Indian War over North American lands

1763—England, victorious in the war, gains Canada and most other French lands east of the Mississippi River

1764—British pass Sugar Act to gain tax money from the colonists

1765—British pass the Stamp Act, which the colonists despise; colonists then hold the Stamp Act Congress in New York City

1766—British repeal the Stamp Act

1770—British soldiers kill five Americans in the "Boston Massacre"

1773—Colonists dump British tea into Boston Harbor at the "Boston Tea Party"

1774—British close up port of Boston to punish the city for the tea party

1774—Delegates from all the colonies but Georgia meet in Philadelphia at the First Continental Congress

1775—**April 19:** Revolutionary war begins at Lexington and Concord, Massachusetts

**May 10:** Second Continental Congress convenes in Philadelphia

**June 17:** Colonists inflict heavy losses on British but lose Battle of Bunker Hill near Boston

**July 3:** George Washington takes command of Continental army

1776—**March 17:** Washington's troops force the British out of Boston in the first major American win of the war

**May 4:** Rhode Island is first colony to declare itself independent of Britain

**July 4:** Declaration of Independence is adopted

**December 26:** Washington's forces win Battle of Trenton (New Jersey)

1777—**January 3:** Americans win at Princeton, New Jersey

**August 16:** Americans win Battle of Bennington at New York-Vermont border

**September 11:** British win Battle of Brandywine Creek near Philadelphia

**September 26:** British capture Philadelphia

**October 4:** British win Battle of Germantown near Philadelphia

**October 17:** About 5,000 British troops surrender at Battle of Saratoga in New York

**December 19:** American army goes into winter quarters at Valley Forge, Pennsylvania, where more than 3,000 of them die by spring

1778—**February 6:** France joins the American side

**July 4:** American George Rogers Clark captures Kaskaskia, Illinois from the British

1779—**February 23-25:** George Rogers Clark captures Vincennes in Indiana

**September 23:** American John Paul Jones captures British ship *Serapis*

1780—**May 12:** British take Charleston, South Carolina

**August 16:** British badly defeat Americans at Camden, South Carolina

**October 7:** Americans defeat British at Kings Mountain, South Carolina

1781—**January 17:** Americans win battle at Cowpens, South Carolina

**March 1:** Articles of Confederation go into effect as laws of the United States

**March 15:** British suffer heavy losses at Battle of Guilford Courthouse in North Carolina; British then give up most of North Carolina

**October 19:** British army under Charles Cornwallis surrenders at Yorktown, Virginia as major revolutionary war fighting ends

1783—**September 3:** United States officially wins Revolution as the United States and Great Britain sign Treaty of Paris

**November 25:** Last British troops leave New York City

1787—On December 7, Delaware becomes the first state by approving the U.S. Constitution

1788—On June 21, New Hampshire becomes the ninth state when it approves the U.S. Constitution; with nine states having approved it, the Constitution goes into effect as the law of the United States

1789—On April 30, George Washington is inaugurated as first president of the United States

1790—On May 29, Rhode Island becomes the last of the original thirteen colonies to become a state

1791—U.S. Bill of Rights goes into effect on December 15

# INDEX- *Page numbers in boldface type indicate illustrations.*

## About the Author

Dennis Brindell Fradin is the author of more than 100 published children's books. His works for Childrens Press include the Young People's Stories of Our States series, the Disaster! series, and the Thirteen Colonies series. His other books are *Remarkable Children* (Little, Brown), which is about twenty children who made history, and a science-fiction novel entitled *How I Saved the World* (Dillon). Dennis is married to Judith Bloom Fradin, a high school English teacher. They have two sons named Tony and Mike and a daughter named Diana Judith. Dennis was graduated from Northwestern University in 1967 with a B.A. in creative writing, and has lived in Evanston, Illinois, since that year.

---

# Photo Credits